Love, Loss and Cardiac Issues

impspired@gmail.com

Cover artwork by Poppy M.E Brill

ISBN: 978-1-914130-81-6

Love is all you need

- *The Beatles*

OTHER TITLES BY IMPSPIRED

Out of the Chrysalis –
by Mary Farrell

Unplugged -
by Robbie Taylor

Classical Adaptations –
by Susie Gharib

Irish Hares & Seahorses
by North Coast Writers

The Taste of Your Music –
by Sarah Mackey Kirby

Cracking the Air –
by Jimmy Milliken

Periodic Stories Volume 3 –
by Jim Bates

IMPSPIRED

Introduction

By Steve Cawte

Love, Loss and Cardiac Issues is a book of many things. Its contributors come from across the globe and it shows that no amount of distance can keep us from having to deal with some of the challenges that make us all human.

What struck me most about this book was the amount of material that flooded in to me, so quickly after announcing the intention to publish. Everyone has a story to tell. Everyone has been touched by loss of some kind. But throughout all of the material, even those that seem most bleak, it is the love for that person that drove it. The loss hurts, but only because of the love, the trauma is only so hard to take because of the love, the pain, so hard to bear because of the love. And, as time does it's thing and allows us to not forget, but to contain those heightened feelings of hurt, the scales tip and we are left with more of the positives. Can see beyond the darker moments and remember the joy and happiness. The fond times, the memories made – the love.

This book is specifically designed to raise funds for cardiac research. It is a cause that is close to my own heart, cliched pun intended.

Contents

Howard Debs

Summers with Aunt Sissy

"May their memory be for a blessing"
Jewish honorific

His name was Mel, a traveling
salesman. He almost always
smoked big cigars and he had
a big car. In boyhood I didn't
pay much attention to things
like make and model but it
all fit just right; there he sat,
puffing away on his stogie,
cigar smoke fleeing out the car
window which he rolled down
all the way, his left arm resting
there his left-hand dangling,
holding the steering wheel
with his right, heading towards
Grand Rapids with me along for the ride.

She was there to greet me
through how many summers I
can't recall. There were sleep away
camps back then, but those were
for the snooty kids from neighborhoods
where I didn't ride my bike. When I
was older, I remember going to day

camp at the "Y" each camper wore
a tee shirt with the camp name
on it so the counselor could keep
track of us on field trips, but before then,
it was summers with Aunt Sissy.

Mel worked with Uncle Bill, each
had a territory to cover, so mostly it was
me, my cousins, and my aunt, for two
maybe it was three weeks that I stayed.
I lived in the city, in Chicago, so
back then the visit was like going to
the country. I played outside, thinking
back, there was lots of open land nearby
where I'd conjure up all kinds of fantasy.

Then it was dinner time. She'd call me
to come in and made sure I washed my
hands. She'd ask if I had fun, if I enjoyed
being away, and I'd say something childish
in reply and she'd answer "now you tell me"
she said that all the time. Those were
special days, except for the cottage
cheese and peaches, canned I guess,
or the cottage cheese and pears she
served it seemed with every meal. I don't
like cottage cheese and fruit but that's
about the only thing I don't think
of fondly to this day.

In memory of Sariece Rubin, (1926-2022)

Danny Best

Danny's Prayer

when that long awaited for moment
finally finds its way to my bed

suspending itself
just barely…just briefly
to pause beside my weary old head

I would ask only
that my passing may come
as a friendly compassionate guide

in the untroubled deep…of a calmly night
to collect my spirit…from where I abide

and to silently still me
away to home

on the wings of every memory
of every love…I've ever known

Just A Thought

If you should find yourself
wondering

'am I really…really there

right there with you
everyday

"yes"

of course I' am

there in your heart
and in your memories

no matter where in sleep I lay

if you'd really like to talk
but you feel there's nothing left to say

then please…please

lighten-up that heavy…heavy…heart

'cause

I'm really…really…only
just a single thought away

Mark Blickley and Francesca Schwartz

Pumped Up For Next Gig

Oh wow. Oh wow. Oh wow.

Last words of music I-pod creator Steve Jobs.

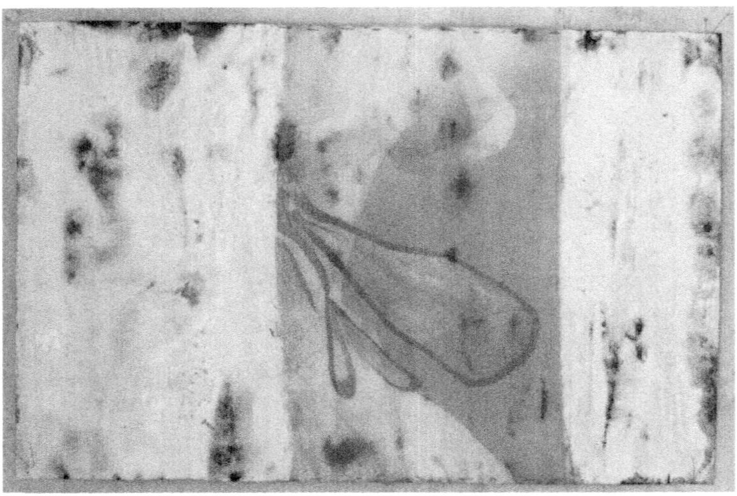

Painting "Arrested Heart" by Francesca Schwartz

I don't remember any of my previous incarnations. This one just ended with the sound of my heartbeat replaced by booming defibrillator jolts. I can hear being zipped into thick plastic but I am not afraid. Aimless transmigration drifting will play no part in my future.

I don't understand why I came back as a drummer, an impoverished, financially unsuccessful percussionist ridiculed for a passion that labels me a bum, a perpetual adolescent, irresponsible and selfish. But creating music by pounding on those stretched skins until they vibrate me into mysterious intervals of bliss is an addiction I never want to kick. I've never considered myself religious or spiritual at all but now that my gig has ended, I realize I spent my 47 years on earth as a priest. I cannot define this mystical bliss. When words and intellectual thought cannot describe a thing, it's called a mystery. That's why they created the word God. God is a musical term for irrational explanations of sacred truths.

We are all born musicians. At the time of my inception, Mom's heartbeats were the first organized rhythmic sounds I heard. Four months inside her womb I joined her with my echoing heartbeats, and then I pulled away to create my own unique beats and rhythm.

Musica Humana. Bookended between the first beat I heard from my mother's heart is the final beat I heard from the artificial rhythm of a defibrillator, tuning me up for my next incarnation. It's a much slower, angrier beat. When it couldn't tune up the instrument called my body, I am discarded. Defibrillator is electronic music—a no-no for true musicians who spurn the use of living drummers in favor of techno-drum machines. Defibrillators, not Schoenberg or Stravinsky, are responsible for the atonal music of the spheres.

Mom hated me becoming a musician. She said I would end up poor, drug addicted, a wasted life. Yet she loved music and streamed it so often it most certainly inspired me to take up drumming. I've never felt closer to her as when I replicate her heartbeat with my sticks. Every time I pounded or brushed those skins, I now see I was paying homage to my mother and the in- utero cadences she bestowed upon me.

As a drummer, I am the heart of a band's rhythm section. Heart arrhythmia are irregular beats which I've done plenty of times on stage and while jamming with other players, though I called it musical experimentation. Strange how we never know during our life how often we are rehearsing our death. My heart arrhythmia is genetic. The same musical rhythm from Mom that gave me life also killed me.

All lives are musical compositions and decompositions. Does the tune end abruptly like a song at a live gig, or does it fade away through artificial manipulation, like a recorded song that doesn't know how to end so it keeps getting fainter and fainter until it slowly disappears? Should one just keep going as long as mechanically possible or should one issue a DNR directive in order to cease and desist? Sound waves never truly disappear, they just keep getting weaker and weaker until they transform into thermal energy units, which are eternal. That is the true definition of human harmony we call soul music.

There is no single moment of death, but a series of mini-deaths. Hearts continue to beat after breathing stops. Skin cells remain alive several days after death so we can trade in our worn drum kit for a fresh set of skins. It's a reverse audition where the drummer doesn't try to get accepted into a group, but decides to join a new human group with which to ignite innovative and invigorating percussive riffs.

There is a white light at both ends of this tunnel, but they are simply stage lights that can really be a pain in the ass when performing. I pound my way through them even though it's hard to see fellow band members and my audience. But this white light has dark shadows sprinkled within and these are musicians hoping I will jam with them in our next life. I am sandwiched between the white theatrical lights of past musical performances and future ones, as I inch closer to a new incarnation and my next gig.

Margaret Royall

OUR BITTER-SWEET SUMMER IN FRANCE 1998

The cow dying in the nearby field was probably a bad omen on day one. Hardly had we settled into our holiday home in south west France than shouts of anguish from outside assailed our ears. We rushed outside, faces radiant with summer holiday expectation, only to be greeted by a couple of desperate farmworkers in the meadow trying to haul a sick cow back on its feet with ropes. All attempts to save the animal were in vain and we tried to put its ensuing demise out of our minds and get on with the serious business of enjoying ourselves.

I had a degree of unease in my mind, knowing that these two weeks away had been booked in the hope of helping my husband recover from a serious heart scare and what the medics were now labelling post traumatic depression. The idea of sunshine, relaxation, swimming in the pool, exploring our favourite area of France had seemed to be just what the doctor ordered! The good life awaited us; past trials could be forgotten. At least that was the hope.

It started well enough (apart from the cow incident!) We soon discovered a charming village nearby with bakery and supermarket, perfect for our everyday needs and in

the opposite direction a small market town nestling on a hillside crowned by an ancient castle with crenelated tower and walls. It was a haven for artists, poets and craftsmen of all kinds, a vibrant village, basking in the sweltering heat of the midday sun. It would prove our favourite spot, somewhere that could open us up to the possibilities of an exciting alternative lifestyle
with its abundance of cafes, bistros and market stalls selling merguez sausages, ratatouille pizza slices and the like. The sheer joy of sipping kir in the shade of a bougainville epitomised for us the Good Life in France.

My husband seemed more relaxed, was able to sleep better, gradually started to regain his appetite. We were both huge francophiles, enjoying gourmet dining as well as the simplest
meals in the humblest of local cafes. Wine was his greatest love though and our summer holiday jaunts usually included several visits to the local vineyards, culminating in a compulsory 'Degustation' and the purchasing of as much fine wine as our car boot would hold.

"I think I must have a problem with my sinuses," my husband said one day. "I feel like I've got a heavy cold, a lot of pressure in my forehead."
"Don't worry, I've brought the Olbas oil," I said, fetching the medical box I always packed for a holiday. "Boil the kettle and put a few drops in some hot water in the basin, then put a towel over your head and breathe in the steam. That should help."

It did initially, but worryingly the pain kept returning. The intense heat which only abated in the late evening and early morning hours certainly wasn't helping. Usually he was a sun-
worshipper, turning a glorious shade of brown at the first hint of exposure, whereas I would easily turn lobster red even in a short time and needed factor 50 sun cream! This year, however, he shunned the sun and seemed reluctant to stay outdoors at all for very long.

More concerning, however, was his continuing confusion and disorientation. There were only two possible ways to go when exiting our property; basically, right to the village and left to the castle on the hill.
"Which way now?" He looked quite haunted and desperate. I was a little annoyed and almost snapped back, "What's the matter with you? Surely you know where the village is by now?
He was crestfallen, like a child put down by an insensitive teacher. Sadly, this confusion became worse over the following days, accompanied by a diminished appetite, a disinterest in what our teenage boys were doing, even avoidance of going in the pool. I tried to get reassure myself that it was just the depression but I secretly started counting the days to our departure. The final straw came when we had popped into the village by car. On the drive back he shot straight past our property.
"Stop, stop! What on earth are you doing?" I shouted. "Turn round and go back, you've missed the house!"
He seemed not to understand but started to back up – and straight into a ditch! Luckily it was a shallow one and

we managed to get the car out in one piece. It left me shaken though and concerned as to why he was doing these strange things. It was so out of character. Yet he himself seemed totally unaware that anything was amiss.

To try and reduce my stress-levels I took to meditating and spent time doing psychic exercises every morning, (having been recently told I definitely had psychic ability!) We had always planned to retire to France and a further reason for visiting the area this year was to look around for a suitable property. Early on in our stay we had visited an estate agent and been taken to view various possibilities. 'Les Cailloux' was the one! It was a remote renovated barn with fantastic potential. It nestled in a green valley, it's red tiled roof shimmering jewel-like in the glaring afternoon heat. How thrilled I was therefore when the interpretation of one of my psychic exercises seemed to clearly indicate that November was going to be a month of huge impact. Everything I had experienced during a deep meditation fitted the details of the place; close to a river - yes, trees shading the plunge-pool – yes. That had to be it, I thought. We would surely become the proud owners of this gem in November? At last, my long-cherished dream of owning a bolt-hole in France was going to be realised! I was delighted.

Once back home from France it was time to celebrate our younger son's birthday. His choice of meal was a Chinese takeaway and my husband asked me to go with him to pick up the order. We drove round the corner of our lane onto the main road but then, unbelievably, my husband steered straight into a row of parked cars! There was a loud crunching noise. I grabbed the wheel in panic and steered us back on course. "Sorry, sorry," said my husband. "I didn't see any cars there. I don't know why." This was not good. Deep within me I recognised at that moment that there was a serious problem. Perhaps he had suffered a stroke? I thought, reflecting how in recent months he had shown a tendency to veer to the left when walking and when driving in the outside lane on a dual carriageway had sometimes wandered over into the inside lane. However, a subsequent visit to the optician revealed nothing major. Maybe I was fretting unnecessarily.

My birthday loomed large in September and I was curious as to what I would receive as a gift this year, (my husband not being noted for his appropriate choice of gifts!) My daughter pulled me aside early on in the day and I could hear the concern in her voice.

"Dad couldn't write your card properly, Mum, I had to hold his hand and guide the pen! "What is the matter with him, Mum?" "I'm not sure, but I think we should take him to the doctors immediately. Something's not right here," I said, shaking my head.

I fetched him back from work, where his secretary reported that he had withdrawn to his office, shut the door and fallen asleep. The twenty minutes spent with the GP will be forever etched on my memory. Our GP was also a personal friend, which made things all the more difficult for all of us. Questions were asked to ascertain his ability to recall information and name well known objects. The doctor pointed to his tie and asked for its name. He stuttered and stumbled through a few disconnected syllables, greatly distressed and trying desperately to recall what he ought to be saying. His responses became more ludicrous: Who was the Prime Minister? - Lionel somebody! (At the time it was Tony Blair.) Which day followed Monday? - February! The GP avoided eye contact and suggested sending him for an urgent brain scan.

Perhaps the worst ever day of my life followed a week later. I couldn't get my husband in the car to go for his hospital appointment. This man, renowned for his sartorial elegance, had put on a dirty shirt and stuffed a shredded wad of toilet paper in the top pocket of his jacket! I was horrified. Now running late, he decided he needed to eat breakfast, which he brought out to the car. My attention was diverted from this as I went to open and pin back the double gates. Quickly jumping into the driving seat, I set off. Crack! I had driven over something. Slamming on the brakes I got out to investigate and to my amazement found a cereal bowl shattered to smithereens under the wheel. The tyre was deflating, air whistling from the gash. At that point, I have to admit, I lost it completely, running round the yard, hands clasped to my head howling in despair. Oh, how I needed the comfort of another human-being, a friendly face, someone to take charge and help me out of this hell-hole! But of course, nobody came.

Finally, we made it to the hospital where he had the brain scan. We were put in the day ward and would be seen by a senior neurologist as soon as possible. I recall the blank walls and the striped curtains blowing in the breeze at the open window opposite. An elderly lady, who was recovering in the next bed, shot us a sympathetic look.

"Is your hubby ok? He looks like he's seen a ghost or something," she remarked.

At that very moment a serious male nurse appeared and took us through to what I remember as a staff rest room. I recall a microwave oven and people heating up drinks and food. It most certainly was not a suitable place to take in the grim news he was about to give us! He held up the scan and pointed to a dark shape clearly visible on one side of the brain.

"There's an abnormality here," he said.

"Well...... what is it?" My voice almost failed me.

"It would suggest a tumour," he replied in a matter-of-fact manner. "But you need to see the consultant for a full diagnosis."

I knew in that instant it was something terminal and the blood drained from my face. My heart pounded in my chest and I gripped the nearby chair to prevent myself from fainting...

There followed two months of horror and dark distress, the precise details of which my brain has thankfully chosen to eradicate almost completely. There were stays in hospital, grand mal fits, a complete loss of speech on his part and the ability to stand and walk unaided. Then a

terminal diagnosis. He had a brain-tumour, glioblastoma grade 4, untreatable. I was told this in a matter-of-fact manner by a specialist who was totally devoid of any bedside manner or empathy.
"Take him home to die," was his final pronouncement before hastening from the room.

Two months later the bitter-sweet memories of France had faded and autumn leaves were already falling. On the twelfth of November my beloved husband died peacefully in our local hospice with me at his bedside. One week later, as I stood at the graveside, clutching a single red rose in one hand and the quivering fingers of my fifteen-year-old son in the other, it suddenly struck me..........November! That psychic prophecy! How wrong could I have been?! Instead of acquiring the keys to our bolt-hole in France I was burying my husband.

Day Trip to the Beach

The Mind is willing but The Flesh is weak

I watch them on the beach below,
disabled younsters on a day-trip to the coast,
burrowing their starfish limbs in the sand,
searching for mislaid dreams in rainbow rock pools.

Clumsy fingers grasp spades and dig down,
eager to retrieve lost selfies, filling buckets with regrets
for a life they can only dream about.

Sun hats blow off in the gusting wind,
sailing across the shingle like drunken seagulls,
their owners squealing with pure joy.

Cotton-wool clouds unfurl their bushy beards,
release virtual ladders in response to the laughter.
I watch the young faces tilt skywards with misplaced
hope.

Today is a reprieve from institutional boredom,
an invitation to fantasise about alternative lifestyles;
yet in reality it's simply a vain idyll, sadly forever
beyond their reach. Their faces say it all.
If only...

Susie Gharib

My Love in Red III

I saw you row our zestful friend,
the spectral boat that had been dead
for three decades since it was wrecked.

Though thrilled to stroke the harbour's breast,
the reluctant oars began to gape
at a single tear that scarred your face.

You headed north then further west.
The sun had sunk without a trace
and a wind in gusts began to rave.

I sat at the edge of an awkward bed
bewailing the only friend I had,
my rosary, burning drops of blood.

I couldn't kiss the clay that lay
wound in white for worms to hail,
the flame, departed from the slain.

Years of grief appeased no gods.
A one-way journey, despite my sobs,
had claimed the man and a floating cot.

I breathe the words I used to hear
from him who left behind his dreams,
all soaked in red, slaughtered and maimed.

Snowfalls in Spring

Now the face is all fissured
And the heart is so disfigured,
Why should pain be all mirrored
Before Age its fields has ploughed?

The charts those tears had left
Are maps of joys bereft,
Of a heart so early cleft,
And hopes whose flames went out.

The lightning my forehead streaks
In branches down cheeks it sneaks,
Delves deep to the heart it seeks
And heralds snowfalls in Spring.

Crest

A Scottish breeze
would bring some ease
to the grieving oak
and what it weeps
for falling leaves
would never cease
to whirl to where
he lies in peace.

The space he leaves
will hurt the leas
where your thoughts have grazed
for thirty years,
but words he breathed
into your ears
will blow the sails
that crest your seas.

J.S Watts

Morning Song

I am feathers and flowers,
iron and rust,
the red of the rising sun as she is torn
between sky and earth,
maker and made,
the song and the singer.
A half-life clawed back
from human-kind's detritus.
Abandoned evening junk
reclaiming dawn's existence.
Never young,
but not old enough
to float on the wings of history
into yet another iron-clad morning
that will, inevitably,
spear the day
to its solid steel core.
Scraps of rags flutter
in the morning breeze.
Let time begin, continue, repeat.
The heart's optimism always
conquers reality.

Sherry Shahan

Lingering

I am four-years-old. Sitting on the edge of the porcelain tub while my mother paints on her cat-eyes.

It is not enough to watch her in the reflection of the tri-fold mirror. I want her to face me, to feel her arms around me, to squeeze me until bedtime. Instead, she sprays her sweeping up-do with Aqua Net.

Eight-years-old.

I still wait.

Now I want to tell you about my mother's rabbit. It died when she was sixteen. But that's a misnomer since all rabbits tested died. A few days after being injected, the female is sliced open. Ovaries change in response to hormones secreted by a pregnant human.

Twelve-years-old. I have stopped waiting.

But I want my mother to tell me the lie that everything will be okay.

I am seventeen. My rabbit dies.

My mother's tears gather on her cheeks.

~

I am thirty-two. My mother and I come together over the evening news and a cocktail, adult conversations, book-ended with laughter—returning to the same stories, family history relived, reorganized, rewritten.

In the memory, she smiles at me. This is why the memory sticks.

Let me tell you about the first day of spring eight years ago? When sunlight reminds me of children reciting a nursery rhyme.

~

My mother lounges on the loveseat beneath the living room window. She chose the plaid fabric from Sears, her favorite go-to department store. She is hooked to an oxygen tank, shrunken inside her fake-velvet jogging suit, her cat eyes deep in a trashy paperback, living her last moments like clouds in an ever-changing sky.

~

I am in my sixties, standing in the driveway of my mother's home of sixty-four years.

My mother's beloved lemon tree is lifeless. Her clay pots, cracked, shriveled roots exposed. No bees or butterflies.

Her hushed voice presses the silence. *Does any part of us remain here? Does a house begin to settle in on itself when abandoned? Is it the breath of the occupants that hold it up?*

But first I want to tell you about my stepfather of forty years. Lost. Lonely. Vulnerable.

The family fears he has become a host to a parasite who has oddly become executor of the estate and co-signer on bank and retirement accounts. The parasite buys a $90,000 Tesla, registered solely in his name.

While hosting this organism my father loses fifty pounds and dies alone on an autumn day when every branch is leafless.

The parasite drives away.

~

I want to tell you about the house, empty, the air stale, unable to exhale. A door slams for no reason.

There are alternatives to what I am doing. They just do not interest me.

~

The parasite nailed a second curtain rod above the front window and hung a thick red blanket; a veil of dull dust, deception and danger.

I climb onto the loveseat in a crossroad of time, sorrow quivering through my bones, and lift the curtain rod from its bracket. Afternoon light bores through the window in flaxen triangles. I am reminded that this is the only time of year when sun touches the deepest crannies of the living room.

I sit on the brick patio under my mother's orange tree, planted so she could bag fruit for family and friends. Because this tree is alive with blossoms I stretch my fingers and keep stretching them, knowing healing begins on the uppermost branch.

Douglas Colston

Speculation, cogitation, conjecture and theory

'Seizing an opportunity for benefit or profit'
(speculation)
is like a trebuchet
(or any other weapon that throws stones),
'carefully thinking things over'
(cogitation)
may involve supposition, surmising, speculation or conjecture
and 'theory'
(a coherent idea that explains observed facts
and correctly predicts new phenomena)
could be considered synonymous with doctrine
(a tenet of philosophical matters).

Criticizing, scolding or upbraiding
learning or knowledge
is deep advocacy or promotion
of lamentation and grief
well-acquainted with
the workings
of the heart and mind
that has been abandoned.

To discard the heart and mind
is like a deep sleep ...
thoughts, feelings and moods

that promote, advocate and reason
predict, expect and anticipate
understanding, realization, learning, knowledge,
teaching, instruction, training,
happiness and delight.

Infer – make a judgement …
fixing, settling or arranging
makes principles.

Estimation, assessment, reckoning or consideration
scatters and disperses
so that conceptualization
is fundamental.

Thinking, planning, intention,
discussion, talk or debate
that initially calms oneself
is the beginning.

RP Verlaine

For Adele and The Duke

My girl
sweet sad eyed Adele
a mermaid of pleasure
I drowned in too often
to treasure breath,
came to me in crying.

Bowie had just had
a heart attack.
"He's so young
it just can't be
what if he dies"
she kept repeating.

The details came slow
as a hospital drip.
Our Ziggy
the thin white duke
living master of the image
in flux/had fallen during a
concert in Prague.

Adele was beyond
reason saying she'd take
her own life. At one point

I had to twist a sharp knife
from her hand before news
came Bowie would live.

Later, more heart attacks
would follow before cancer
drew his velvet curtain to
a close 14 years later.
When I lit a candle and
played his last record-
Dark Star.

Contact with Adele
severed for years
Bowie's music kept her
close as that long night
his heart would not surrender to
as I so held Adele close
so hers too would keep beating.

James Mulhern

Leaves

That fall day we raked leaves from behind the shed.
Smell of earth and wet decay rose in the cold air.
We could see our breath.

Worms and beetles scattered through a fence.
I saw dirt and thought we had finished.
"Not yet," you said.

The gray sky grew darker and the wind chilled.
When your flashlight showed not a speck of leaf,
You said, "We're done."

Today I look at the wet leaves below.
I kneel and clear your grave.
Again, I smell the earth and feel the biting cold.

The damp leaves shimmer like tears, not many,
that drop on the yellowed grass.
"We're done," I hear you say.

I say a prayer, cross myself, and rise.

I see my breath and imagine I see yours.
I should leave, I think, but not yet.

"Arise and Go Now"

I arrived at Rita's house about noon. Her blue eyes widened when she opened the door. She patted the sides of her red hair and smoothed her pleated cotton nightdress, a pattern of honey-bees. She was always donning unusual clothing or changing the color of her hair, which was ash blond a month ago.

"Aiden, I'm a mess. I fell asleep on the couch. Come in." She held a book entitled *Audrey Rose*.

She saw me looking at the cover. A girl in a red dress stood in front of a grave. The ground was on fire.

"Junk. I hope you're reading better things in school. . . What grade are you in this year? Old people lose track of time. The years merge together and sometimes they seem to disappear." She laughed.

"Ninth."

"Before I know it, you'll be in college." She rubbed my

head. "Let's sit in the backyard. It's such a lovely day."

We walked through the hallway and kitchen to a brick patio covered by a pergola. She led me to a black wrought-iron table. Sunlight flickered through the red cedar lattice above us, dappling her face. The air smelled grassy and pungent. Cat urine? Then a scent of roses reached my nose.

"Will ya have a cup of tea?" She pulled out a rusted chair.

"Sure."

"Sit here. I'll be back in a jiff."

A blue jay lapped the greenish water of a fluted cement birdbath, then shook its wings, cawed, and flew away. Along one side of the patio, potted plants moved in the breeze; a few swayed in macramé holders—lush ferns, the yellow and green spider plant, the wandering Jew with its purple and green heart-shaped leaves, and some I could not name. Children laughed on the other side of the tall hedge. Hanging on the fence was a metal plaque with a quote my grandfather recited during one of his mysterious visits: "Goodness is the only investment that never fails."

"Come grab the door." Rita elbowed the screen door. She held a small tray with a teapot, two cups, milk, and sugar. As I hurried towards her, a chipmunk darted in front of me.

"Thank you, Aiden."

When we were seated, she said, "Isn't this peaceful?" She looked around. "Sometimes I sit here from morning until evening, watching the birds lift their wings or listening 'til the crickets sing." She laughed. "That rhymed. I'm a poet." She poured tea into a cup with milk and sugar. "Here you go." Then she poured her own. A small pot of azaleas cast a purple glow under her chin.

"I want to apologize," I said.

"For what?" She sipped and looked at me over her tea.

"Nanna and I lied to you."

"And when did you do that?"

"I don't have leukemia."

"I know that, Aiden," she said matter-of-factly.

I began living with my grandmother when my mother was admitted to McCall Hospital, a psychiatric facility near Boston, the year before. My mother's claim that she heard voices of dead people and her frequent 'visions of past and future events' led to a diagnosis of schizophrenia. My mother believed that the passing of time was an illusion and everything was happening all at once.

Nanna was granted guardianship of her, and me as well, because Dad said he couldn't handle children on his own. My brother Martin went to live with Aunt Clara a few streets away. The judge thought separating us would ease the financial burden for our extended family.

Nanna had taken me to see Rita, her closest friend, a few weeks earlier. She told her that I had leukemia and asked for help with the medical bills.

"If you knew my grandmother was lying, why did you write the check?"

"Your grandmother is a lifelong friend. She needed money. I recognized her anxiety and wanted to help."

"Aren't you mad?"

"Of course not. Catherine lies." She looked away. "But we all do. To others and to ourselves." A shadow passed over her face. " 'Life is a tale of human frailty and sorrow.' Do you know who said that?"

"Shakespeare?"

She smiled. "Good guess. But it was Nathaniel Hawthorne in *The Scarlet Letter*. You'll read the book in high school." She scrutinized my face. "You're not here to talk about school. To what do I owe the honor of your visit, dear Aiden." She put her elbows on the table and rested her chin in her hands.

"What was that book about? Not *The Scarlet Letter*. The one you were holding when I came to the front door."

"It's about a man who loses his wife and daughter in a terrible car crash. He's heartbroken, so he goes to a psychic to get solace."

"What does the psychic tell him?"

"She tells him that his daughter has been reincarnated as Ivy Templeton, a girl living in New York City. He sets out to find her, but you'll have to read the book to find out what happens."

"Tell me."

"It would ruin the surprise. If we knew endings, life would be mundane, don't you think?"

My hand shook a little as I drank the tea. "You sound like Grandpa."

"How do you know what Sean sounded like? He died before you were born."

"Rita, do you believe there's life after death?"

"I tend to think not."

"Do you believe in ghosts?"

"I've never seen one, and I don't know anyone who has." She sipped.

I was quiet.

Furrows appeared in her forehead. "Have you seen a ghost, Aiden?" She laughed and put her cup down.

"Maybe."

"Either you have or you haven't. Which is it?" She reached across the table and grabbed my hand. "Tell me about your ghost. I love stories."

"My grandfather."

"Sean?" She sighed. "Oh that it were true. I miss your grandfather so very much."

"Ghosts are true."

"Aiden, you have an active imagination."

I must have looked annoyed.

She smiled. "I believe you *think* you saw Sean's ghost. . . . Don't be angry with me." She poured more tea into my cup. "Shall I get you some cookies?" She was about to get up.

"He came to me at night. He said my mother doesn't belong at McCall's and we should help her escape. He told me to ask you for help because you always know what to do. You fix things."

"Aiden, your mother's ill. You were dreaming about your grandfather."

"He said my mother isn't crazy." I looked down. "And neither am I. He told me we both have 'second sight.' "

Her eyebrows raised, her face pale and serious. She moved her chair to my side of the table and put her arm around my shoulder. "Ya know what I think?" Her eyes shone kindly. I smelled whiskey. "I think you have a creative mind and you should write stories. The Irish are known for their literature." She threaded my hair with her fingers. "You've got his hair. And you're so much like him with your curious ways." She patted my knee. "Help me clean up." She rose and placed our cups on the tray with the teapot. "Run ahead and hold the door open."

"He wanted me to thank you for helping him find my grandmother's pearls. He said he laughed at you for praying to Saint Anthony before you went to the car. You found the necklace between the seats."

She dropped the tray. Bits of blue and white china smashed on the bricks. A cardinal swooped down and sat on the birdbath.

Her shoulders trembled. She pointed to the birdbath. "That was your grandfather's favorite bird." She wiped tears from her cheeks.

I felt awkward and stooped to pick up the mess.

"You'll cut yourself. Sit at the table with me."

The cardinal flew to a cross-beam above us and looked down, as if it were listening to our conversation.

"How did you know about the necklace? Did you read something in one of your grandfather's journals?"

"I didn't know my grandfather wrote in journals."

Her chin jutted forward and she fingered her collar. "Aiden, I'm trying to discern how you learned these things. Sean and I were the only people who knew about the pearls." She smiled, looking upward at the cardinal, lost in a memory. "Did he tell you why he was giving your grandmother the necklace?"

"No."

"It was their first anniversary. Your grandmother was due home any minute. I had helped him prepare a nice dinner—filet mignon, green bean almandine, baked potatoes, and a fancy salad with croutons and anchovies. He went to his closet to get the pearls and came back in a panic. I prayed aloud to St. Anthony. He laughed at me, but when I returned from the car, he was joyous."

"Do you believe me now?"

She covered her lips with two fingers and stared. "Maybe. . . . I suppose anything is possible."

The cardinal swooped in front of us and flew away.

Rita touched her chest. "That bird scared the bejesus out of me."

"Will you help then?" I said.

"Help what?"

"Rescue my mother."

Rita twisted her lips and pondered. "We've got to ask Margie to assist. We need more than the two of us." Margie was another of my grandmother's friends.

"I already did. She agreed. Martin did, too."

Rita put her hand on mine. "Okay. We'll meet here to come up with a plan." She looked at the clock. "You better leave. Your grandmother will wonder where you are. You mustn't tell her anything. She's stubborn."

"My mother is visiting from the hospital."

"Why are you here, Aiden? You should be spending time with your ma."

"Nanna took her to church."

Rita laughed. "I'm sure Laura was thrilled. And on a Saturday, too!"

"My mother doesn't agree with the church. She said they screwed it all up once Saint Paul and Saint Augustine got involved."

"I was kidding. I know Laura was never one for organized religion. But she's a good daughter. Trying to make your grandmother happy. You and your brother come here after school on Monday. Where is Martin now?"

"Probably swimming at the YMCA. Then back to Aunt Clara's."

When we were at the front door, Rita said, "I'll call Margie. You speak with Martin. Will fried bologna sandwiches do? I know how you boys like those. Your grandfather's favorite." She smiled.

"Any food is good."

She opened the storm door. "Hurry along."

I ran down the steps and turned once to look at her. She waved, wiping more tears from her cheeks. I thought how great is the power of love and memory.

Rita was frying bologna when Martin and I arrived on Monday.

"Grab the mustard from the fridge." She used a knife to cut a dollop of butter off the stick. It sizzled in the pan and the bologna smelled delicious. My mouth watered.

"The two of you look hungry." Her lipstick was a brownish tint. She was wearing a blouse with a brocade design of a lake, and purple bell-bottom pants. "A new fashion" she would say, when she saw Martin and I giggling at her outfits. Her forehead perspired and she daubed it with a paper towel. Several gold bracelets jingled on her arm.

She looked past us, down the dark hallway towards the front door. "Margie is always late."

"It's 'cause she never goes anywhere," Martin said. "Probably takes her a while to get out of that chair." He laughed.

"That's true. Suffers from a broken heart, but I wish she'd get over it. Arthur was the love of her life."

"Who?"

"I told you the story, Martin," I said. "Remember her high school sweetheart?"

"Oh yeah. The guy that dumped her when she got fat."

"How was your time with your Ma?" Rita said.

Martin and I looked at one another. He nodded for me to tell her.

"It didn't go so well."

She used a fork to place a piece of sizzling bologna on a plate next to the stove, then pulled the meat off the tines.

Wiping more sweat off her forehead, she turned to face us. "What happened?"

"She fell from a tree and broke her arm."

Her eyes fluttered. "What was she doing in a tree?" She turned the burner off and brought the meat to the table. "It's self-serve," she said, motioning to the bread, mustard, and bologna.

Martin said, "She was helping a girl get down."

"Who was the girl and what was she doing in your grandmother's tree?" She laughed.

"There was no girl," I said. "Not a *real* girl. A vision. She said the girl was wearing a green pinafore, whatever that is. Her scarf was caught on a branch."

"What the Christ are you talking about?" She looked at each of our faces.

"She *thought* she saw a girl." My jaw quivered, as I made sandwiches for Martin and me, then passed the plate of bologna to Rita.

She turned to Martin, who was staring at her gold barrette.

"Do I have something in my hair?" Rita touched her head.

"I like how that metal thing glimmers."

"Thank you."

"I think the girl was a ghost," I said.

Rita frowned and sighed. "Where is your mother now?"

"She's back at McCall Hospital."

"And what about her arm?"

"It's with her, too." Martin laughed.

"Stop being a wiseass or I'll poke you with this fork." Rita raised it in the air.

"Nanna says it was a hairline fracture. Mom has a cast, but she'll be okay." I bit into my sandwich.

"Glory be to God. Catherine must be at her wit's end."

The doorbell rang. Rita stood. "Not a word about your mother's fall to Margie. She doesn't know when to keep her mouth shut. She might say something uncharitable to your grandmother." Rita walked to the front door.

"She wears the craziest clothes," Martin said.

We heard Rita say, "You shouldn't live holed up like you do. You're not a mole."

"I like moles." Margie laughed. "Got a few in my yard."

Rita and Margie entered.

"You boys look like you're up to something." Margie frowned and placed her handbag on the table. Rita moved it to one of the counters.

"Sit down, Margie." Rita pulled a chair out. "We're having bologna sandwiches. Help yourself."

"Fancy schmancy." Margie plopped onto the seat. Her bum hung over the edge. She wore white spandex and a red sweater over a blue t-shirt. I thought, Why do fat people always wear sweaters?

I made her a sandwich.

Rita announced, "So what's our plan?"

"I'm nervous that we'll get in trouble. I gotta pee. Be right back," Margie got up.

When she returned, she said, "Sorry about that. Good thing they came up with adult diapers. I wear them all the time. Seems I always got to pee. When I get nervous. If I sneeze or laugh. Even when I fart."

Martin put his sandwich down. "That's appetizing."

"Honey, it's a fact of life. Older people lose control of their bladders. I saw on TV that astronauts wear MAGs during liftoff and landing."

"What are MAGs?" I said.

"Maximum Absorbency Garments. Something to do with gravity makes the astronauts have to go. I have a whole different perspective of John Glenn. Can't seem to get the diapers out of my mind when I look at him."

Rita tapped the end of her knife on the table. "We're not here to talk about urination and the United States Space program."

"*Urination.*" Margie smirked. "Rita, you make everything sound so intellectual. The way I figure is we all shit and pee. Nothin' to be ashamed of." She took a bite of her sandwich. Mustard smeared on her chin. Rita scrubbed the frying pan in the sink. "And women, Aiden." She tilted her head in Rita's direction. "Their bladders drop after a certain age. I bet hers has plunged," she whispered.

"What? They just fall out of their you-know-what?" Martin laughed.

"Wouldn't that be funny?" She pointed at the white linoleum. "Lady, your bladder's on the floor. Watch your step." She slapped her thighs. Her bum wiggled.

"Enough!" Rita's face was pink. "Let's discuss our plan to

get Laura home."

"We can bring her down the back stairwell. Rita, you wait in the car so we can make a quick getaway. The three of us will go in."

"What about the security guard who sits by the door?" I said.

"That guy loves hearing stories about buses and the MBTA. I told him Dad worked for the T last time we were there and he ate it up. I'll distract him while you guys sneak out. Then I'll follow."

We finished discussing our plan. Rita brought us to the front door and waved when we reached the sidewalk.

A few days later, we drove to McCall's. Rita said it was best not to tell my mother; she might inadvertently let on that something was up.

The day was brisk. Leaves had begun to explode into their autumnal brilliance—vivid shades of red, orange, and yellow. Through the open car windows the scent of dying leaves wafted into the small space of our car. The lyrics of Chicago's "If You Leave Me Now" played on the radio.

As we approached my mother's unit, my stomach grumbled from uneasiness.

The three of us—Margie, Martin, and I—checked in at the nurse's station.

The receptionist, a college-age girl with purple nails and feather earrings, said, "Can I help you?"

"We're here to see my mother, Laura Glencar," I said.

Nurses, doctors, and aides walked up and down the hallway. A janitor emptied a wastebasket into a large bin on rollers. The girl called on the intercom for Nancy, my mother's nurse.

"Hello." Nancy smiled.

"We're here to see Ms. Glencar. These are her boys." Margie tugged on her sweater.

Nurse Nancy said, "I was just in her room. She'll be so happy to see you. Go right down."

My mother sat up on her bed and extended her arms. "Come here, boys."

Her hug was warm. She kissed our cheeks repeatedly. Her red blouse smelled like cinnamon.

She looked up. "Margie, it's been a long time. How are you?"

"I'm alive."

Martin said, "I'm going to the restroom." He winked at me.

"The bathroom's right behind you." My mother pointed.

"That's okay. I saw one by the entrance." His forehead raised as he glanced at Margie and me.

When he left, I said, "We're getting you out of here."

She stood. "Great. I'm sick of this place. . . When?"

"Now."

She jumped up and quickly threw her things in suitcases. Before we left the room, she pulled the emergency cord from the wall. Lights flashed and a high-pitched sound blared.

Martin had succeeded in moving the security guy away from his post at the door to the stairs. Two nurses ran into my mother's room. The security guard said something into his radio and rushed towards the commotion. Martin held the door open. "Quick."

My mother's laugh was infectious. Our laughing echoed

in the stairwell. Margie moaned, easing her fat body as rapidly as she could down the steps. I called to her, "Hold the railing. You don't want to fall."

Mom raised her cast. "You'll end up with one of these."

"I don't think they have one for broken asses." Margie breathed heavily.

As we exited the building, Rita honked the horn. We hurried across the lawn. The car doors were open.

"Hurry. Get in the car," Martin said.

A chubby security guard and Nurse Nancy bolted around the front corner of the building. "Ms. Glencar, you can't leave." She held up her hand. "Grab the patient," she said to the guard. His shirt was wet under his arms and his pale belly was visible between buttons.

My mother said, "Okay. Okay. We wanted to go outside for a bit." She looked up. "Isn't the sky lovely? And look at that dove in the tree."

"Dove?" The heavy security guard looked at the Maple tree. My mother kicked his shin.

"Fuck. That hurt." He hopped, holding his leg.

"Not as much as staying in this hellhole." She escaped his

grasp and was almost seated in the back of the car when a black sedan with two additional guards blocked Rita in.

"Lady, you're not going anywhere," one shouted from his window.

Rita got out of the car. "Why can't the young woman go home?" she said to Nurse Nancy. "The children need their mother." She was wearing a black pantsuit with a beret, as if she were starring in a spy thriller.

Nurse Nancy walked over to my mother and whispered in her ear, guiding her towards the entryway of the building.

"It will be alright," Mom said to us. "Go home. Visit again soon." She tried to sound cheery, but I felt her sadness. She waved before entering.

We heard a cooing sound. On a branch, a grey mourning dove fluttered its wings. Beyond the tree, on the lawn, I saw my grandfather.

Margie said, "What are you looking at?"

"The dove."

Rita stood silently, her eyes watery.

"Everything will be alright. Someday soon, we'll all be

home," Martin said.

We were quiet as we drove to Nanna's house. Martin looked out the window to avoid my eyes. I think he was crying. Occasionally, I saw Rita watching the both of us in the rearview mirror. I felt a pit in my stomach, anticipating my grandmother's reaction. Nurse Nancy would certainly call her.

When we pulled in the driveway, Rita said, "Let me do the talking."

My grandmother was sitting on the couch, pretending to read the newspaper.

"We're sorry, Catherine."

She didn't look up. Her lips were tight and her eyes were red from crying.

"The boys just want their mother home."

Martin and I sat in two wingback chairs on the other side of the room. Margie went to the bathroom. Rita stood in front of the glass-topped coffee table that separated her from my grandmother. "Won't you say something?"

She folded the newspaper and threw it at Rita. "You think

I don't want Laura home? That I'm a mean old bitch who just loves that her daughter is in a nuthouse?" Her fists were clenched. "You always have to be the heroine, Rita. The *kind* one, the *nicest* person." She snickered.

"That's uncalled for, Catherine. I was trying to help."

My grandmother threw up her hands and sat on the couch. She rolled her eyes. "Yes, Rita. You're always trying to help." She sighed.

Martin and I exchanged glances.

Nanna continued, inhaling on a cigarette. "I love my daughter. And I hate that she is stuck in that God-awful place."

Rita circled the coffee table and tried to hug her. My grandmother pushed her arms away. Rita stumbled, knocking the glass top onto the floor. It broke into pieces.

"Grandpa wants Mom to come home," I blurted. They looked at me.

"I don't understand," my grandmother said.

"He told me."

Martin stared and shook his head.

"That's impossible. He's dead." She extended her arms

along the top of the couch. Martin moved closer to me.

"He visits."

"What in the hell are you talking about?" my grandmother said.

"Sometimes he comes to me at night."

"Aiden, lots of people have dreams about people they've lost," she said.

"Nanna, Grandpa wanted me to tell you it wasn't your fault that he died."

"Of course, it wasn't my fault." She puffed on the cigarette, eyeing me suspiciously.

"Then why do you cry at night and ask God for forgiveness? Grandpa says he's in the bedroom with you. He told me to tell you he was 'full as a bingo bus' that night. He's sorry."

Martin laughed. "What's that? A bunch of old people on their way to play bingo in a church basement?"

Nanna's face whitened and she tapped her cigarette on the ashtray.

"Where did you hear that expression?"

"What does it mean?" Martin said.

"It's an Irish saying for very drunk," Rita said.

"You would know," my grandmother said, looking past her.

"He told me that you should stop blaming yourself for leaving him in the chair when you went to bed. It's not your fault that he choked on his vomit."

"That's gross," Martin said.

Margie entered, wiping her hands on her pants. She sat on the loveseat.

My grandmother shook, tears on her face. "Your grandfather and I had been arguing. He was drunk. I left him in the chair. I should have made him come with me."

Rita sat next to her.

"Rita wouldn't have left him. She would have done the right thing. Taken him to bed with her," she said to the rest of us.

"What's that supposed to mean?" Rita said.

"You know exactly what it means." Her voice was low and firm.

"You kids should probably go upstairs," Margie said.

"They're old enough to hear what I have to say,

Margaret."

"And what is that?" Rita stared, her face rigid.

My grandmother paused and spoke calmly. "That you're a whore. And you sleep with married men." She inhaled and blew smoke. "I'm sure Sean thought you were a good fuck."

Margie stood; her legs wobbly. "Oh my God! Boys, you really need to go play or somethin' "

Martin pulled me from the couch and guided me upstairs. When we were seated on my bed, he said, "Well that was a nice end to the day."

We both laughed, then sat quietly for a bit, staring into space.

"Do you think I'm crazy, Martin?"

"How so?"

"What I said about Grandpa."

He put his arm over my shoulder. "Nothing crazy about you, brother. I believe you."

"I don't want to be put away like Mom."

He looked straight into my face. "Listen to me, Aiden. No one is ever gonna mess with you as long as I'm around.

I'll kick their ass. If you say Grandpa visits you, then Grandpa fuckin' visits you. If anyone has a problem with that, they got me to deal with. . . Remember what I always say?"

" 'I will always have your back,' " I answered.

"That's right, Aiden. That's right."

After that day, my grandmother looked at me differently. Fear? Did she think I was schizophrenic like my mother? One evening, she sat on the living room couch and looked through an old photo album.

"How did you know those details about your grandfather's death, Aiden? I told everyone he had a heart attack because I wanted to protect his reputation." Her words slurred and she held a glass of whiskey.

"I told you, Nanna."

She closed the album. "Stop with your malarkey. Ghosts don't exist." She touched her throat; it had begun to redden.

I sat next to her.

"What does he look like?" she said.

"He has dark curly hair and thick black-framed glasses."

She puffed on her cigarette. "You've seen photographs. . . . What else has he told you?"

"He said Mom has second sight like your mother, who fell down a well."

Her leg trembled against mine.

She turned away. "Go to your room. I can't talk about this any longer."

"Nanna, don't be mad."

"I'm not mad, Aiden. I just can't understand." She rubbed her temples. She picked up the album, preoccupied with a photo about halfway through the pages.

"I don't understand it myself." I walked towards the stairs.

Lost in thought, she didn't hear me.

Nanna had left for work by the time I was dressed and ready for school. I had fifteen minutes before I needed to leave, so I went to the couch and opened the frayed black cover of the photo album. I flipped through the pages filled with old black-and-whites of Nanna's family in

Ireland. When I reached the halfway mark, I scrutinized the images. Nanna's expression when she had looked at that photo was one of anxiety. Why would an old picture have that effect? And which photograph?

Pasted to a faded black page was a paper with writing. Someone, I suppose my grandmother, had copied a poem by William Butler Yeats—"The Lake Isle of Innisfree."

I will arise and go now, and go to Innisfree,
And a small cabin build there, of clay and wattles made;
Nine bean-rows will I have there, a hive for the honey-bee,
And live alone in the bee-loud glade.

And I shall have some peace there, for peace comes dropping slow,
Dropping from the veils of the morning to where the cricket sings;
There midnight's all a glimmer, and noon a purple glow,
And evening full of the linnet's wings.

I will arise and go now, for always night and day
I hear lake water lapping with low sounds by the shore;
While I stand on the roadway, or on the pavements grey,
I hear it in the deep heart's core.

Underneath it and continuing onto the next page were five photographs, yellowed with age. "Our Trip to Innisfree" was written in cursive above the pictures.

Three girls and a boy, my grandmother and her siblings, sat in a small rowboat on a lake. The photographs must have been taken by their parents in a boat behind them. The boy, tall and skinny, wore suspenders and a scally cap, his shirt buttoned to the top of its round collar. He grinned as he held one of the oars above his head. The girls, who appeared to be in their early teens, one perhaps younger, were dressed in old-fashioned dresses. They were laughing at something he said. I spotted my grandmother immediately. She was at the back of the boat, looking towards the island, half of her face visible, a scarf over her head. In each photograph, the island appeared closer. The boy was rowing in the latter pictures; only the backs of the girls' heads were visible, hair cut short, thick locks curling inwards. In one photo, my grandmother draped her hand into the water.

In the final picture, my grandmother was halfway up a pine tree, her scarf caught on a branch. Her brother, looking very serious, reached for her. She looked panicked as he grabbed her stockings and she clutched the branch entangling her scarf.

So that was a pinafore, I thought. Because the photo was black and white, I couldn't tell if the dress was green. I slammed the album shut, grabbed my backpack, and ran to the bus stop. My mother had seen my grandmother in the pine tree on the day she fell and broke her arm. *Time is an illusion.*

The next weekend, my grandmother and I went to McCall's. Martin was at swim practice. Nurse Nancy smiled. "Laura is doing great. She's been busy drawing. Quite a talented artist."

"She gets that from me. I studied at the Louvre in Paris," Nanna said.

"Really?" Nancy cocked her head. She led us down the hallway.

My grandmother asked, "You think I'm too dumb?"

Nancy laughed. "Not at all. It was a stupid thing to say." She turned. "I didn't mean to offend you."

"No offense taken. Next time I'll carry a paintbrush."

"Here we are," Nancy said outside Mom's room. She smiled at me. "I bet you're excited to see your mother."

"We're good now. You can go," my grandmother said.

When she left, I said, "I didn't know you were an artist, Nanna."

"Don't be silly, Aiden. That was blarney. Nancy Nurse is a bit too uppity for my taste." She pushed me forward. "Go in. Your mother will be so happy to see you."

"Hi Mom," I hurried to her bed, where she sat drawing in her sketchpad. She wore a green gown that accentuated her eyes.

"I want to eat you up." She kissed my face and hugged me tight. "I've missed you so much. There's no one to talk with at this place." She looked past me.

"Aren't you going to give me a kiss, Ma?"

"You need to visit with Aiden. I have to speak with the nurse. I'll be back soon."

My mother asked about my favorite subjects in school, my grades, my teachers, and did I have a girlfriend.

In a few minutes we heard loud voices in the hall. "I'm taking her home, Nancy Nurse. I'm her mother and I was appointed guardian by the court. Haven't you got a bedpan to empty?"

They entered the room.

"Let me get in touch with the psychiatrist on call."

"That won't be necessary. Nothing he says will change my mind. . . Laura, get up, dear. We're going now. You're free."

"Please give me a few moments to collect the paperwork, Mrs. Mulroy. You need to sign her out A.M.A. That means against medical advice."

"I know what it means. I'm a nurse, too. Do what you must."

My mother and I were already packing her suitcases.

"I'm sorry for bringing you here," my grandmother said to Mom. "You should be home with Aiden and Martin."

Nanna signed the necessary forms and we left. Before getting into the car, both my mother and I saw him. My grandfather was sitting on the grass beneath the tree. He smiled and waved to us. A star shone in the twilit sky.

"Hurry up, slowpokes," my grandmother said, then turned towards the Maple. "What are you looking at?" She followed our gaze.

"Hope," my mother said, laying her arm over my shoulder and guiding me into the backseat before closing my door.

When they were inside, I said, "How can you *see* hope?"

My grandmother started the car and looked at Mom. "Hope is sitting right beside me."

Mom touched the back of my grandmother's neck. The car moved forward.

I opened my mother's sketchbook. An image of a painting fell out. She had begun copying it, using different shades of pencil. A blindfolded woman in a green gown sat atop a light brown globe, her head bent to the left. She played a lyre with a single string. In the background, one star sparkled in the gray-blue sky. Printed underneath the reproduction was "Hope, 1886, George Frederic Watts."

I thought of the poem about Innisfree and the photographs in my grandmother's album. I rolled my window down and imagined I heard crickets singing.

After a while, my grandmother said, "I've got to make a stop before we go home."

"Where?" my mother said.

"Rita's house."

"Why?" I asked.

My grandmother looked at me in the rearview mirror. "Aiden, what I said to Rita last week was cruel. I humiliated and embarrassed her. I need to apologize. Do you understand?"

"I do."

My mother kissed my grandmother's cheek and leaned against her shoulder.

In my mind, I saw the picture of my grandmother as a panicked young girl in the tree. A brother rescued her, Martin would always rescue me, and we had just rescued my mother. At this very instant, people throughout the world were helping one another. I reclined, listening to the low sound of wheels on the pavement. My mother was free. In a sense, my grandmother was also free. In my "deep heart's core," I knew everything would be alright. Soon we would all be home.

Jim Bates

The Drive Around Phantom Lake

"Nicki, look," Frank pointed. Dust billowed as he slowed the car to a stop. Out on Phantom Lake about one-hundred yards from shore were a pair of trumpeter swans and their four young. "See how white they are. Big, too. Aren't they beautiful?"

Frank was taking his time driving up the west side of Crex Meadows, a thirty-thousand-acre wildlife refuge in northwestern Wisconsin. He had driven to the area that morning from their home in Orchard Lake, Minnesota, a three-hour journey, just to see birds in their fall migration. It was mid-September and already the oaks and maples were turning rusty red and orange.

Frank pointed again, becoming excited. "Look at all the ducks. I can see blue-wing teal, redheads and shovelers." He peered through his binoculars and added, "There's also some common mergansers farther out and a few golden eye. Bufflehead, too." He smiled, "That's very cool." He silently gazed over the big lake, a half mile across and a mile long, a well-known stopover for hundreds of thousands of waterfowl feeding and resting on their long flight south for the winter. He was enthralled.

After a while he put the car and gear and continued at a slow pace, stopping frequently to watch the ducks, dipping and dabbling in the calm water. Overhead bald eagles and red-tail hawks soared in a robin's egg blue sky.

A movement to the left caught his eye. "Look, Nicki, there's a marsh hawk," he pointed, "And a sharp-shined, too." Both raptors were gliding over the marsh grasses the area was named for, Crex being short for carex, the grasses common in the huge wetland and at one time used to make rugs.

He drove on. "You having a good time?" he asked. The loop around the refuge was seventeen miles of gravel road and he was enjoying puttering along, moving slowly, pointing out clusters of sandhill cranes feeding in nearby corn fields, various songbirds, more eagles and hawks and even some osprey. It took two hours to make the circuit and he loved every minute of it. He was sure Nicki did, too.

The end of the drive took him past a modern looking visitor center remodeled ten years earlier with donations from the one-hundred thousand visitors to the refuge each year. He and Nicki had generously contributed and had become friends with many of the staff.

Frank parked and walked through the front door, glancing to the right into a small office. His friend Bob

Jensen was at his desk working on a computer. He was the game warden for the area including the refuge. "Hi, Bob," he called, waving.

Bob grinned and walked out to greet him. The two men shook hands, "Good to see you, Frank. Beautiful day, isn't it?"

"Can't beat it. But give me a minute, will you?" Frank held up one finger and shuffled his feet. "I need to use the little boys room."

"Go for it," Bob smiled.

On his way back, Frank joined Bob who was talking to a high school girl running the cash register in the gift shop. The three of them chatted for a few minutes about the waterfowl migration before Frank said, "Well, I'd love to talk some more but I've got to hit the road. Long drive ahead."

"I'll walk you out," Bob said.

Outside, the scent of pine was pungently pleasing in the warm, late afternoon sun. They walked quietly until Bob touched Frank's shoulder and said, "Say, before you leave, I just wanted to say how sorry I was to hear about Nicole. I couldn't make it to the funeral last spring, but I was thinking of you both. That congestive heart failure is a bitch. I guess her old heart finally just up and gave out. That's too bad. She was a great person; a fine lady."

Frank laughed, "What'd you mean, Bob? She's doing just fine. She's great."

Bob just stared at the old man, bent with age, withered with not only arthritis but also the years. He decided not to push it. "Okay, whatever you say, my friend. See you next year?"

"You bet. We'll be up for spring migration. Maybe even participate in the April sandhill crane count."

"Sounds good. See you then."

Both men shook hands once more. Bob watched Frank get into his car and pull away, wondering if the old guy would even be alive next spring. He'd aged considerably since his last visit. Oh, well… Bob headed inside to the sound of geese flying overhead and crossed his fingers, saying a silent prayer. *We can but hope.*

It was dark by the time Frank got home. He fixed a grilled cheese sandwich for dinner and fed Hootie his seven-year-old tabby cat. The two kept each other company for the rest of the evening.

He began nodding off while watching the ten o'clock news so he got ready for bed. Breathing a heavy sigh, he slid under the covers, lay on his back and stared into the darkness. It'd been a long day and he was exhausted. He felt the kitty cat jump onto the bed and make herself comfortable down by his feet. In a moment he heard her purring. He smiled. She was a good companion. Then he turned to his side, put his hand on the empty spot next to him and said, "Good night, Nicki. What a great day we had, didn't we?" The only reply was the soft purring of the cat.

He pulled the covers tightly around him, happy he'd made it through another day without succumbing to the crushing loneliness he'd felt ever since his wife's death. Each day was a challenge. Each day he did the best he could.

He closed his eyes and drifted off to sleep. Tomorrow he'd get up and face the day. With Nicki's help, of course. With her forever and always by his side, he'd find a way. He was sure of it.

Jyoti Nair

Chaconne!

Dragon wings of nephrite-jade ravines
Garrotte those ankle-filigrees
Carvings of her surreptitious thoracic
Therefore, she is a mutilated Chaconne!
Feet-thrumming…
Rubescent-girdling…
Would you know the incense for her sepulchre?

Torsos of her yearnings trill
Suffocated arched-songs of Eurasian Blackbirds, in tandem
She's the scorched kite-tail
She, the sloughed-off skin-slather
Of melodies embroidered on birch-wrists
Will you write her frayed-poetry today?
Those maggots are nibbling, the lashes of Canis Major
Even as her soul saunters on the outskirts of Sirius…

John Welsh

THE HEART OF THE MATTER

Hearts beating in their caged home.

Home is where the heart is even in if war torn and broken

Broken heart as it did not work out, too much or too less said.

Heartless was the accusation however anatomically incorrect. It is there working fast or slow.

Heart blood being pumped to all organs and limbs to cure pain and aches.

Heartache through grief and worry.

Here I sit so broken hearted, paid a penny and only farted.

A hearty breakfast sets you up for the day.

Each day a heart to heart will clear the way

Unchain my heart and let me live free again.

Ann Christine Tabaka

Heartbreak

Every heartbeat   tells a story
of want and need
      or love and loss

Every breath   expels a longing
for another day
      upon this earth

So many moments
So little time

Tears trace a river of desire
reaching out   to touch a life

We live in quiet desperation
      placing time upon a shelf
            placing it safely
                  out of reach

Hoping   beyond hope
that someday   it will be there
      for us to keep

Peter Magliocco

Gazing at the Vandalized Space

Much is open in the sieve

My knife made in your heart,

Beautiful crimson rivulets gushed

In the honeyed arteries sauntering

Through some transfused flesh.

I sat wondering, alone

In your hospital bedroom then, gazing at

The relic of your vandalized space –

Once housing memories of your life –

Now a transplanted sanctuary becoming

Monstrance memoir of your rhyming lies.

Far from easy dalliance,

Into your cream-paling chest I sought

The sonnet rending, no longer being
The hallowed host of your salvation.
I paused, curious, watching you suffer
From the blade you paid a fortune for,
As you wallowed into a sanguine sinkhole
Where only the damned see themselves wholly
Again, in a piecemeal resurrection
Of a thousand crucified private parts
Later made public on the world-wide-web;
Each lusty blood droplet a shimmering void
For a silent shout to our dying love.

The Still Unwritten

When the best of everything rattles the infinite jest

& nothing's funny anymore, we're born into the radiance of the void.

Whatever smacks of everlasting deliverance, I beseeched

Doctor Divine not to turn me away, just to give me

One more proverbial chance.

Sure I've screwed up in life, all the little embarrassments

Keep ringing amber alarms in the mnemonic mind games

Each day wastes in me,

Remembered sentences never written down:

Severed thoughts mired in life's waste-bin still haunt

The backlit roads of memory

We never want to travel again.

Chuckling ruefully, Doctor Divine just laughed (frowning

At his computer screen

& muttering choice imprecations)

While getting my personal file ready for the judges.

Again I begged him to listen to my sad story,

My remonstrance for having embraced evil

With the aplomb of a fascist functionary.

I wrote poetry while the capitol burned

& the proud rioters did unspeakable things

Raping the heartland of its beauty:

Despoiling the land Frost held sacred, I wrote poetry

Of jarring nonsensical lines my reason

Rebelled against, even damning me

After each comma and pathetic period, yes;

I wrote just poetry, Doctor Divine, though I too

Raped something in myself & others:

Feeling whatever walled us into

The makeshift moronic wend of existence

Rendering humanity fit for the bolus bags

I write the truth still unwritten now,

A final love letter to the fates – & you,

In that immaterial vastness of another wasteland

For all the heartless angels damning me.

DC Diamondopolous

1929

Douglas Haines was not an impulsive man. He'd given it a lot of thought—his decision final. He stood atop the Savings and Exchange Bank in the financial district of Los Angeles. The wide box toes of his oxfords suspended over the roof's ledge. Ten stories high, with no awning to catch a leg, the sidewalk empty, there would be no question of death.

He looked across Spring Street. The new city hall building dwarfed the Barker Brother's Furniture Company, Coulter Dry Goods, and every structure downtown. Giant candy canes and fake laurel were fastened to street lamps. Outside the post office a Santa Claus rang a bell over a donation pot, shouting, "Ho, ho, ho, Merry Christmas," mocking Douglas, who'd lost everything in the stock market crash.

Without money, how could he give to charity? There'd be no Christmas tree, no presents for his wife and daughter. Merriment had disappeared with his fortune.

He blamed the bankers, the stockbrokers, himself. Greed had grabbed him by the lapels. He remembered the seductive breath of it urging him to acquire more capital and with it the insatiable appetite for power. The country was drunk with wealth one moment, bankrupt the next.

If only he'd acted! The warnings of a crash had been threatening. First the September market crash in London. The papers promised the Rockefellers and Morgans would save them—*invest.* And there were his nightmares, for over a week, the same one. He was back in the war, in France, clawing his way through the mud to reach the Savings and Exchange Bank. With each handful of sludge, he slid further into an abyss. He'd wake up shaking, his nightshirt soaked. Mary would stroke his face. "It's just a dream, darling."

After the crash she reassured him that money didn't matter as long as they had each other and Lilly. How could she understand? She who was sheltered from the responsibilities of being a husband and father, supporting a family, protecting them, and if required, going off to war. What kind of man was he who had to send his wife and child to her parents' home in St. Louis—and borrow money for the train tickets from his father-in-law?

Now his gut acted up, repeated stabs that sometimes

reached his chest. *Mary. Lilly. Hard to finish—thoughts, when . . .* he took a deep breath and found strength in taking charge of his death, a semblance of the person he'd been when supervising hundreds of men.

On the 8th floor below, he'd cleaned out his office—pictures of Mary and Lilly, pencils, pens, letters, awards, his pipe and tobacco, a photograph of himself smiling with the moving picture star Buddy Rogers at the ribbon-cutting ceremonies for Mulholland Highway. His life's work was packed in boxes, sealed against a future, neatly stacked, with all the edges touching, for Douglas Haines was a tidy man.

The Great War made him that way. His Springfield was cleaned, uniform buttons polished, everything in tip-top shape. Orderliness lived with him even as he stood on the mantel of the Savings and Exchange Bank: hair combed, shoes waxed, suit pressed.

In 1918, he'd wanted to desert—the bombs, grenades, pissing his pants from the fear of it. He endured but returned home, broken. Now as he gazed out at the dying bruise of a purple and yellow sunset, he *was* deserting. He had no money. A bum. Douglas was more afraid of living without honor, a name, a plaque on his office door announcing his achievements to all who entered, than stepping off a building.

He inched his shoes further over the ledge. Surely death would come in an instant. Then what? Not even the Carnegies or Vanderbilts knew the answer to that.

He saw derbies bobbing along the sidewalk. Where were the men going? Home? To other rooftops? That damn Santa ringing the bell. How come the sun sets—the moon rises? He looked up. There must be stars out by now in St. Louis. Had Lilly made a wish on the first one? He closed his eyes. Teetered.

He grasped his chest, leaned his upper body back. His left hand felt wrong. His thumb rubbed an empty space where his wedding ring had been—best ten years of his life. After he'd packed up his office, he left an envelope on his desk. Inside it he put his wedding band and wallet—also, a note to Mary telling her he loved her and Lilly, and that he was sorry. Would she understand? And Lilly. A child needs a father. His body twitched. He was back in the war, felt the dank mire of the trench, shooting at the Hun, men dying, scared and homesick, longing to run away.

Steady, Haines, he told himself. Find courage in being, a—a what? A coward?

"Mary," he whispered.

He'd met her after the war. She brought everything that was good and clean and kind into his life, turning his dark world into one of wonder and hope. Then Lilly came. "Daddy's home!" Every night she'd run into his arms. It was the best tonic for a hard day's work. Who could love them more than he did?

He blinked, a hood of darkness flung over his future—never to see his child or hold the woman who brought him back to life. What would they think if they saw him standing on the edge of a building? How would his wife feel if she found him in the morgue? Could they ever forgive him for deserting them?

Douglas Haines was not a crying man. But tears for his family came hard, like a torrent. He took out his handkerchief and wiped his face. He stepped down from the ledge and crouched against the side of the building, shaking.

He stood, brushed off his suit, made certain his tie was centered and straight, then walked across the rooftop to the door and opened it.

Sarah Mackey Kirby

The Sky Keeps Us from Falling

When a heart weakens, it works harder.
Counterintuitive, maybe, but it's true.
The more failing and tired it feels,
the harder it works; the bigger it gets.
We share a sky, all the big-hearted
folks. A sky so wide that when we
lie in summer grass and look up,
we know we're all below the same
expanse. Some of us see blue.
Some, gray. It changes day-to-day
and place-to-place. But we know
the colors connect, all over. They

crash into one another above a Texas
food truck, selling street tacos during the
lunchtime rush. And the wispy cirrus
clouds join their ice crystals above
lush Kentucky farms, acres of green,
horses standing strong before their dawn
workout. And above the UK and France.
Canada and India. Ecuador and Nigeria.
Australia and China. Jordan and Haiti. The

oceans, somewhere above the oceans, where
countries cease, where dividing lines
can't reach. In the spaces that make us one,
the colors connect there too. Morning peach.
Sparkling gold. Rinse-through blue
come together. As one sky. One big
fat sky. Like one big old struggling

heart, larger than it should be.
Not strong, but working harder
than it should be. And we know.
This mess of big-hearted folks,
we know the terror and strangeness.
But none of us is alone. We share
a sky, a sky that stretches farther than
we see. Joining stains, bridging storms,
collecting clouds, connecting stars
and constellations. Connecting breeze.
Across the world, all these beat-down hearts.
Above the salt from seas and tears, we link
our dreams. Our breaks. Our nations.

Prayers and Ticking Monsters

I'd prefer if you left me out of your prayers today.
You can pray for me tomorrow. For my
heart, my next surgery, whatevs…and only
if you don't let me know you are. Matthew
6:5-6 says, you should pray in your closet.
I just can't take uncloseted God this morning.
I'm less tolerant before my coffee
has kicked in and when my azaleas
are dropping petals like it's hot.

I've prayed before. A lot.
I prayed to find my husband, only that guy's
not at all who I got. My prayer was
for someone more book-talking,
less football-watching, more culture-y,
less socks-on-the-floor tossing.
But I wouldn't trade him. Mine's a keeper.
He stays with me through all this hospital
stuff. When my chest and wits have had
enough, but this hell doesn't seem to stop.
If you say I got him because God knows better,
then why'd I bother to pray for my idea
of a husband at all? If He intended to send me
this Godsend (pardon the pun and word contradiction)
of a man (albeit more hooded sweatshirt-y
than I'd had in my head) to begin with?

The monsters keep me up sometimes.
Clocks, you know. The ticking monsters.

If I were to drift from this earth (that's
a euphemism for you know what), you'd
say, she's with God now. And it's what
He wanted. Well, no thanks. I'm good.
If I stay, you'd say God answered our
prayers. But what of his plan? Honestly, I'm a bit
tired of God's plan for me. I'd rather walk up
stairs and breathe more easily.

Been a lot of praying going on. A lot of attributing
my here-ness to His doing, while giving Him a pass
on all that hurting. To me, God's got some
'splainin' to do. About this pain that if it
truly is His plan, he's caused me and my
family to go through. For FORTY years
(That's not anger; it's emphasis),
especially if He's had the power to make
this hurt end. And if Jeremiah 29:11 is true,
that God "...plans not to harm you." Inaction
is a form of harm. It doesn't make sense. I'm not
salty about all this. I'm really not. In fact, my attitude
and fortitude, and other tudes are pretty darn good.
But I'm not in the mood for prayers this
morning. Their scars make me uncomfortable.

Hope Lives by the River

When I was little, I used to name everything,
the squirrels, the trees, the butterflies, my favorite mug.

Along the Falls of the Ohio River, where the fossil beds
lay in limestone, somewhere in the mess of driftwood

that moved along the shore of shale, was this rock. Some
rock that
was probably once an ancient marine creature, now
forever

embedded like a scar into the landscape. I can't remember
what she looked like or why she stuck out to me. But I
know

I knew she was a she. And I knew to name her Hope. If
I'd
try to find her among the thousands of other old rock
creations

today, I'd be looking forever. But I know she's still there,
marred but with us somehow. Stepped on and lined with

years of summer storms. Analyzed by
paleontologists, eager
to discover what makes her unique, how history brought
her

to this place. Hope still lives by the river. She's always,
always there.
Among spillway wash and layers. Time-carved and
facing the sun.

Linda Imbler

Universal Sorrow

Loss,
such a small word,
but conveying the greatest sense of heartache.
Who among us
has not had the experience
of huge pain
at the loss of a person, place, or thing?
Traumatic, tragic,
in many instances senseless.
Some get through it with effort,
find recovery.
Some never will.

It is the universal sorrow,
Loss.
The one thing affecting all living creatures
other than death,
and even death is that.

The Heart Shoppe

I walk and examine all the shelves of the Heart Shoppe,
and peer into all containers and crates;

I hear owners discussing needs of young men, sadly
weakened by the poverty of loneliness after love fails;

They know what to stock, what dear things to show upon
these shelves; staunch friends, truth in speech, joy, child's
laughter;

I've seen ladies bankrupt in chasms of sorrow, anguished
women whose bodies betrayed them while birthing;

I've viewed hopeful eyes, scanning within, of those
whose choice went wrong, sighting that second chance,
only to be found cash poor;

Cures are sought here for envy, suicide, racism, all at a cost few here can pay;

I've seen souls wage horrific war, I have seen commanders decide which side shall lose the least, they now search for atonement here;

I postpone my own heart's desires, use my full purse to make true the dreams of those betrayed, the ill, the brokenhearted, and old ones;

All those, shopping for cures for grief or adversity, I fill carts, buy them hope,

Their redemption, my peace.

Lisa 'Annie' Harpel

At the Heart of It

(a haibun)

We've been friends since 2001, after I started a job at the gallery where you worked. We came to be part of each other's stories; my bitter divorce, losing mom to cancer, dad to dementia, brother to a tangled illness, your fight with cancer - twice, losing your mom, a close friend, and a cousin. So much loss, so many funerals. Through it all, even after I moved 300 miles away, we remain a phone call or text away. Birthdays, holidays, big news, life changes.

You were married for forty-six years. Shared the same bed, regardless of arguments, differences of opinion. Travel, dinners with friends, time with family was the plan now that you were both retired. Instead, he was diagnosed with dementia. Changes came quickly: his personality, confusion, awareness, falls out of bed, down the driveway. So many falls. You made the difficult decision to place him in assisted living. More falls, an infection, a hospital visit. He needed more care. Another move, to memory care. Now he's under hospice, and you're in Atrial Fibrillation. All this during the height of a pandemic.

unable to be with each other physically
he cries out for her
through the window that connects them
she whispers "I Love You"

Ken Cathers

even though

even though
they had brought me
home from school
      at noon

to tell me
of my father's
sudden, inexplicable
      death

I still found
myself, later
that afternoon

on the front step
waiting
one last time
      for his return.

David Milner

Funeral Arrangement

Denis did the same thing every morning: stared at the contents of his food cupboard, like an actor waiting in the wings for a cue he couldn't remember. Denis wasn't supposed to eat the foods he'd grown up with, all the foods he loved to eat; carbs, fats, salts, and sugar any which way. Not since the heart attack felled him. Not that he'd prepared and cooked that often pre-acute cardiac event; nearest he got was watching Saturday morning chefs on the telly. Staring at the contents of his food cupboard? Healthy option/ pretention to vegetarianism. All part of the after-care plan. A fellow named Phil, from the cardiac rehabilitation team, had pointed him in the direction of online healthy cooking sites – Denis had all the leaflets anyway. He'd learnt how to boil a beetroot, shred celeriac and, (*quelle idee!*) chew his food properly. He was taking long walks for the first time in years, noticing things and places anew; he felt cleaner, as though he'd been dry cleaned then aired in a delicate summer breeze. He noticed ants traversing the bark of trees! His olfactory senses seemed heightened. He didn't feel as bloated, didn't feel as tetchy; people had commented that he was smiling more. He'd learnt all the words to Leonard Cohen's Hallelujah! Yeah, Life was....

The trill from his phone arrested his reverie and took him from the kitchen to the lounge. Samsung at work on the arm of his (has to be said!) brand new sapphire blue velvet sofa.

Ah. Cheryl. Cheryl with a soft C; *have a sherry with me Cheryl?* Cheryl Cantor (hard C) was, to his ears, a strident name, redolent of provincial privileges, steering groups, middle ranking managerial prowess. There were times she scared the life out of him.

"Denis..." Cheryl began.

"You sound all out of breath," said Denis, instantly wishing that he hadn't; especially including *all,* with its suggestion of... what?

"What? Out of breath?" Her voice sharp as a slap across his chops. "I'm getting the kids ready for school, Denis."

It was difficult for him to think of Cheryl Cantor as a mother, mummy.... Oh, boy. The woman was forty years old! "Yes, Cheryl, thanks for calling..." Denis recovered,

"Er, Cheryl…Are you still…?"

"I am. It's going to be a long day, Denis."

The cheek, the cheek of the woman whose surname meant lead singer in a church congregation. A lot to get through, she was saying. Denis pictured what she might be wearing on the morning of this a lot to get through day, a silk robe, maybe not long out of the shower – no sound of her children in the background – maybe in her bedroom… legs crossed at a dressing table.

"Have you been in contact with anyone from the family? Denis?"

She had a liking for black fishnets and black leather, or suede, knee length, zip-up boots….

"Denis, have you…?"

"Yes, well no, not as such…"

"Not as such? What does that mean, Denis?"

"His nephew, Gordon, in his sixties, no-neck bow tie type, Cheryl; Civil Service exec…"

"Okay, Denis, thanks, bit too much information there."

She was using that (oh so) patient tone. Cheryl Cantor was Area Manager for Fairways Housing Group, comprising sheltered and supported housing for alcoholics, vulnerable old souls, low to medium risk mentally ill, which included Olive Tree Lodge, the place Denis had toiled these last ten years. Edwin Hulford (deceased) was eighty-five when Denis had first arrived. And Cheryl with a soft C, striding about the place in her sexy heeled boots wouldn't have known him from a hole in the ground; two years in the job she only knew him by name once he'd popped his clogs! The Cantor woman wasn't known for her sentimentality, which is no bad thing. Edwin was a bag of bones occupying a bed. The old boy wasn't dead five minutes, his little room was being turned over, fumigated, farted-up mattress in the wheelie bin, readied for the next… commodity. Cheryl Cantor was merely following the market (such as it goes for now). Edwin had lived his life. Wherefore the moral weight or metric? The state pension or provision was introduced in 1907, people were eligible at 70, if they lived that feckin' long.

"What's that?" Denis asked as he seemed to have missed the last few items of interest.

"I said, we don't want wreaths."

"No wreaths? It's –."

"Any wreaths received will not be put on display."

"It's… A funeral."

"Wreaths set a wrong tone, we've decided, they're depressing."

"Depressing?"

"For the residents."

"Well…I guess…" Denis didn't have an argument, for, or against; he was blinking at the dark verdant wreath he had bought the previous day from a local florist.

"We'd prefer financial donations", Cheryl was saying, "Or donations in kind. Roses, on the other hand…"

"Or…chrysanthemums..."

"Denis? Are you –?"

"Fine…yes…roses are red." Tears welled in his eyes.

"You're okay with a eulogy?"

"Yep…it's…Got that…"

"You knew him the longest."

He let the tears fall over his ruddy cheeks. He thanked her, "many thanks, for calling." Rang off. He was, in his way, fond of Cheryl, admiring her strength, her no nonsense approach… her brittleness.

He had a desperate need to be liked.

Yeah, in case he should forget, life was the same… turning, each day our daily bread. Could just as easily be tears of joy he was quietly shedding. For the heart specialists, the nurses, the cleaners…for science, humanity…bringing him back from death's door. His emotions running a little freer these days, to be sure. None the worse, if only a little wiser? Bless you all…

Denis, in his tartan-patterned soft velvet slippers, padded back to the kitchen.

He'd have granola and freshly squeezed orange juice for breakfast.

End

Janice Mathis

Candy Hearts Still Break

Do you recall those candy valentines...
those conversation hearts of sugared chalk
were marked with words like You're so fine, be mine?
I want to share a box of those with you.

Perhaps they would remind us of back when,
we said I love you, and meant what we said;
back when our hearts were young and beating fast,
and when we touched each other; passion flared.

Could we rekindle fire between us now?
Are sparks still burning in your heart for me?
Enfold me in your arms and hold me close,
until the rhythm of our heartbeats sync.

To have and hold forever was our vow;
please, Valentine, be mine; I love you still.

Heavy Heart

the things I have stuffed into this
beat up leather heart
I drag around with me at all times
it's weight pulling on my shoulders
impeding my forward progress
yet I grip it with all my power
I can't let go and
I can't empty it

I need these memories,
mementos of the
joys embraced
and pain endured.
They are what has broken me
and re-made me,
they are the glue
that holds me together

Heavy...

yet keeping me strong
as I tug this weight
along with me.
I continue to add
resistance as I
gather more along the way,
more love and
more heart aches,
like gathering wildflowers

to decorate my final resting place.

Only then will I be relieved of
the weight of them...
the things I have stuffed into
this beat up leather heart.

What do these Scars say?

Scar tissue forms over
deep, painful wounds,
sometimes visible, often times not
some on the body,
the worse on the heart

Scars give an account,
of what we've been through,
the wounds we have suffered,
and the pain we've endured.

they serve as a reminder
of lessons we've learned,
when we have been cut deeply,
and when we've been burned.

When a scar speaks to you,
what does it say?
Pain and suffering
have passed this way.

When a scar speaks to you,
What is revealed?
Strength and resilience...
no longer concealed.

Because scars only form
over wounds that have healed.

Kathleen Denizard

Heart to Heart

Ah, the somber feel of love dismissed
Sad days that creep into sadder nights
Not some adolescent rehearsal of a never-ending crush
Empty nights that smear tears on the pillow
And dreams once vivid become faded and lost
Though hearts can repeatedly break
Fractures can be mended
And love found anew
Just as bittersweet forgives and autumn frost and opens
to the sun
In lusty shades of crimson and gold

Tryst

Must have been in early May by the foothill of a mountain,
green as the aspen leaves unfolding
He was coming to the glade, straight on his horse
His hands quivering as wings on a butterfly
Waving and calling my name
Releasing the reins, he stepped down
Wrapped me tight in warm embrace
The curl of his hair dampened with droplets of rising mist,
glowing at daybreak like amber dust,
Fell on his shoulders and then on mine
And I waited, inhaling the moment
When first I kissed him and could not let go
I remember now, it was early May

Remember

Jack stones and Pick-up sticks
Paper dolls and pigtails
You say you don't remember

Football games and campus jocks
Birthdays and presidents
You really can't recall

Though you seem so tired
Your hands are warm in mine

We smile together in the moment
Silent now as the day passes

What to blame for your forgetting?
How to wake that part of you sleeping?

Charlie Brice

A Poet's Heart

For Steve Cawte

To the entrepreneur, the forest is
a trove of toothpicks, but then,
is it still a forest? Where
is the fragrance of pine, the
wind combed trees, the crunch

of leaf and fern under footfall
when finally reduced to a feeble
splinter forced between incisors
after a gristled meal?

What of the organ of life, the symbol
of philia, agape, and eros, reduced,

by some, to the swoosh and rhythmic
fold of an echocardiogram screen—
T waves, peaks and troughs?

Sometimes new muscle is needed
to preserve the persistence of a pump,
but a poet's heart is another matter. It
triumphs over squeeze of tissue, over
throb of blood through veins.

When muscle stills and sinew stiffens,
the poet's heart continues to beat
in every word, line, and stanza. The
heart of a poet pulses the thunder

of language, pervades the hunger of desire,
the placid pleasure or torrid turbulence
of romance, and does so with a rigor
that defies mortis.

Robbie Taylor

LIGHT ENOUGH TO LEAD US ON.

We followed the lanterns,
past the final knot of tree wrapped string,
and made our way into the darkness,
and yet the path we took was never lost,
for you were light enough to lead us on.

We walked in time, hearts held in hands,
keeping tune like marching bands,
for time's a song of castle's fast, on shifting sands,
and so, we sang loud and lustily in to the night,
for you were light enough to lead us on.

We told each other stories, that we once too were told,
of those who's path had started here,
for everyone hopes to find that tree,
for beyond is where the stories end,
and though each step ahead was in to shadow,
it scared us not, for you were light enough to lead us on.

We walked, then ran, and skipped along,
like children. Even when our youth was almost gone,
for even grown-ups taste the moonbeams on their tongue,
and if we had swallowed all the moon could throw,
we would never have missed a single step,
for you were light enough to lead us on.

We had made our beds and slept like winter bears,
and soon we built a larger den,
with room enough for three,
and when we heard our cub crying in the night,
we didn't have to wake the sun to find him,
for you were light enough to lead us on.
And two became three and soon were four,
and still we waited to mature,
for surely only children can laugh until they fill with
light, until they are too bright to laugh some more,
and even when the sun would hide behind a cloud,
we always knew we would find a sunny day,
for you were light enough to lead us on.

And one day I hope, when the moonbeams on our
tongues,
are nothing more than happy memories,
we will once more find the last knot of tree wrapped
string.
And if though those lanterns no longer burn,
we will find our way to help them through the darkness,
for you are light enough to lead us on, you are light
enough to lead us on.

ALL THE THINGS I NEVER WANTED

He opened the door to his cave full of man stuff,
in his Grateful Dead t-shirt, dotted with dandruff,
come on down, he said, I've got some puff,
so, I followed him down the stairs.

He got out the coasters and passed me a can,
we sat beneath posters of superman,
and Pamela Andersen with her Baywatch tan,
comfy chat in comfier chairs.

He asked if I'd seen Lord of the Rings,
and I said I'd seen a lot of things,
yes, he replied, we live like kings,
we're royalty he sneers.

He leans over and puts the needle down,
Thin Lizzy's boys are back in town,
he passes the joint that's turning brown,
washing it down with foreign beers.

We talk about songs we've never sung,
and all the things we've never done,
and he told me then about a blackened lung,
don't you dare, he said, no tears.

He said he knew that God didn't exist,
so why would he spare an atheist,
death's an inconvenience and that's all it is,
there are other things to fear.

He put on Paradise City, by Guns'n' Roses,
and laughed at radiation and diagnosis,
and stiff-armed crucifixion poses,
saying never trust their pinky swears

We remembered when times seemed kinder,
when good old Gazza had played a blinder,
laughing together watching Minder,
making improvements and repairs

The needle scratched on an empty groove,
neither of us could be bothered to move,
the going was rough but the buzz was smooth,
last call for midnight truth or dares.

He said that life can be lived too fast,
that's why we surround ourselves with the past,
that we are only as deep as the shadows we cast,
that life isn't ours, we just buy shares.
He said we're only true to ourselves when we're asleep,
and I tell him a shadow on the lung is pretty deep,
just another memento he says, for me to keep,
he tells me philosophy is cheap,
that philosophy is just remembering other people's
quotes,
it's dinner party chit chat and anecdotes,
because we're all just guests who are taking down notes,
and a philosophers only original words,
are the noises made when they clear their throats,
he says all philosophers are hairdressers splitting hairs..

I look at the boxes of old L.P'S and 45's,
and hidden magazines full of naughty wives,
relics of the lengthening of time and stunted lives,
with their echoes of dull excuses and sharpened knives,
for beneath the gentle touch of a shroud of dust,
sleep the forgotten songs and rotting lust,
where once sat the kings of stick or bust,
not saying the words which are the ones we must.

I reach over and grab an empty beer.
Cheers, I toast,
to the empty chair.
And I smell smoke that isn't there,
hearing the laughter beneath posters of Superman,
and the fading Pamela with her Baywatch tan,
smiling back, as only a sad man can.

You can have all this, he had said, when I'm gone,
every midnight dare and favourite song,
and I couldn't tell him that he was wrong,
that I would never listen to the Grateful Dead or Guns'n' Roses,
without hearing the needle scratch of diagnosis,
remembering that life's too small in bigger doses,
he had told me to take whatever death brings,
because all life is, is stuff and things.

Yes, I reply, into the empty air,
and tip my can to the empty chair,
I close my eyes, and in the darkness,
I realise all the things I never wanted,
are everywhere.

Mehreen Ahmed

Silent Bleat

The sheep floated on the blue, etched on the cloud's sphere. In the short time that I wrote my story in the sky, they had reshaped into vapour, then pelted down. The rain fell over a garbage dump of a used plastic pond. Children of the narrow alley played in the rain as they crossed it precariously over the wavering surface. The only way to decipher a pond underneath, was by the liquid walks of the nimble feet.

Eight, seven, and nine, the children tiptoed. Only their parents knew their names. They were headed towards a destination—a balloon factory. Hired to make party balloons of many colours, blue, yellow, pink, and red, they made a rainbow of balloons and stacked them up in a corner. Balloons, to be used for birthday parties.

They held the rainbow in their palms, but never had the opportunity to use any for birthday parties of their own. After a gruelling shift of making balloons all day, they returned home with a few in their hands. But they flew away. They chased them but they went too high, lost in the sky. Walking the same liquid walk, over the pond, they came back to the alley. Each day, abundant balloons were made to last a hundred parties. They gave hope and joy to the many thousands who were born with a rainbow band around their heads.

The children were soaked in the rain.They crossed the hazardous pond balancing themselves on plastic. The last of the rains withered the lambs away from the blue—a balloon in its own right. The children ran along the alley under this blue balloon. This was a good day, they thought. Because their mothers were home and they could smell the cooking. The four lambs bleated on their respective ratty doors. They cried out—we are home. The mothers let them inside. Their dry mouths spread to hungry grins. Sons and mothers greeted one another.

"How was the day?" mums asked.

"We almost held the rainbow right here in the middle of our palms," they said.

"Meaning?" mums asked.

"We chased some balloons at the plastic pond. But we lost them in the sky, along the way."

"You couldn't bring any home?" the mums asked.

"No. But it doesn't matter," they said.

"Why not?" mums asked.

"Quite simple. We went. We returned. We see you. You see us. What more can you ask for?"

The lambs were back, dissipating once again. This time, they left their signature of the silent bleat in a contrail across the serene blue sky.

L.B Sedlacek

A More Accurate Description of Paint

Dark hues and white. Grays, tans. Blues, greens, yellow, purple and peach. Plain colors. The Amish always dress in plain colors.

That's maybe what she missed the most – her wardrobe or pinks. Maybe some vibrant orange. Neons. Tie dye. Shoes with style. Jeans. Shorts. Sandals.

The plain clothes look was not a look, she thought. But she needed to not be seen, to have no look. She didn't need anyone to look at her.

She had been in Strasburg, PA all of three days working on not standing out, not contacting anyone she knew, not being noticed, not being identified as "English" or non-Amish. She'd even changed her name from Roz to Mabel, a plain simple name. Her hair had been next.

She stared at herself, her hair in the window of the Strasburg laundromat. She looked plain all right. No make-up. A white bonnet covered her un-styled undyed hair. It was naturally brown. She wore a plain black dress, plain black shoes that she suspected once belonged to a man. She shuffled down the sidewalk. The train tooted in the distance.

Among the rolling green hills and valleys dotted with similar farms – all white – the tourist train was a welcome reminder of her past, of her life before becoming Amish.

She slipped in her earbuds and looked down as she walked. The earbuds were white. The looking down pure Amish mannerisms.

She wasn't looking down and listening to music. She was listening to recorded voices of the Amish women she'd heard at meals, services. She'd practiced the accent, her name. she practiced being Amish. She was one of them she kept telling herself. She walked around the town's three blocks four times before someone addressed her.

"Mabel. Mabel?"

She felt a tug at her arm and turned. "Oh. Hello, Mrs. Lapp."

Everyone seemed to share the same last name. It was easy for her to remember names.

"You seemed lost. Thinking of things maybe?"

"Yes, I was trying to remember what I needed for groceries."

The woman addressing her – Rose Lapp – smiled broad. Her face was plain, long dark hair pulled back and stuffed under a bonnet just like hers. She wore black, all black. She was wide, shorter than her. A few years older, too. She'd never dare to ask anyone's age. That was taboo.

"That should be easy enough, dear Mabel. Now follow me."

She did as she was told. She followed the older Amish woman into the country store. It was plain – plain white walls, wooden floors, not even a curtain or blind on the windows.

Inside the small space there were only things people needed – coffee, hot chocolate, breads, teas, hats, gloves, overalls, spices, toys for the kids – simple ones made of wood, cheeses, meats, herbs, soaps, cloth, pasta shells, candies, books on farming, religious books, and nothing more. There were no rag mags – that's what she called the tabloids; the celebrity gossip papers. There were no magazines, either. No free wifi.

The closest thing to her former English life was a newspaper. She stared at the headlines, the front page without picking it up. Three days in and she was still on the front page, but no longer the headline story. Three days in and she had effectively disappeared.

Mrs. Lapp appeared again, she glanced at the paper, tugged her elbow and pulled her away muttering "We have a newspaper we share if you be wanting to read such a thing. Save your pennies. Jacob mentioned you had limited funds."

Mabel (Roz) smiled and nodded. "Yes, that is correct." She thought of Jacob and the three simple colors she'd seen him wear so far (blue, green, yellow.) She thought perhaps the colors all had a meaning, but she knew not what.

She'd just landed on his doorstep and said she related to a distant cousin of his from further up north. He'd been in his driveway on his one-wheel bicycle horsing around. They both knew it wasn't true, but he didn't question it. They both knew she was hiding from the English world she'd come from. He'd only asked her if she was in any trouble. He seemed satisfied with her answer that no it wasn't trouble just she'd lost all direction in her life, she'd hitched a ride from a trucker in New York City and went as far as he'd take her until he stopped in Pennsylvania outside of Strasburg. She'd thanked the trucker and walked until she got tired stopping outside of Jacob's farm.

She thought of her three-day new life and old life all the way back to the farm. She carried two brown paper sacks of goods from the Zimmerman country store.

She walked by the almost identical looking Amish farms stepping as close to the curb as she could get when the occasional tourist car drove by probably looking for the farm or the landmarks from the famous movie filmed in the same parts. She'd seen it, too on a classic movie channel. Liked it.

Would she get used to no TV, no movies, no internet, no news except word of mouth or a newspaper?

He was more reliable than any media source, and he was waiting for her, she knew he would be she thought smiling and pushing the English thoughts, her former life, to the side for the moment. She walked fast and held out the bags to him.

"Jacob. Could you help me with these?"

He nodded and returned the smile. He took both bags from her. She didn't know if she was supposed to ask for help, but she did.

"Mr. Zimmerman put these on your credit. I hope that was okay." She blushed a little as the words tumbled out.

"No mind. He knows I'll make good on it."

"Good. I didn't mean to come here with nothing. It seems I did."

He stepped back and nodded towards the kitchen door. It was plain white, just like the house.

"You are not without anything. I enjoy your company, and your cooking."

She laughed. What could she come up with for their meals today, she wondered. She didn't wonder long and soon he was doing more of the cooking than she was. Roz was not a cook. Mabel was.

Together she and Jacob baked bread, fried eggs and bacon, fixed up a pot of vegetable soup for later letting it simmer on the stove, and made oatmeal. As they sat and ate at a plain square table by the window, he smiled and she smiled.

They were surrounded by shadows and the faint light coming from the window. No electricity. No TV. No phones.

Transportation was a horse and buggy, bicycle or by foot. No running water either.

She carried two buckets in from the well to wash their breakfast dishes. Jacob stood in the corner and watched.

She used soap in one bucket to wash, rinsing the dishes in the other setting them carefully in the wooden dish drainer. Her hands and skin felt dry and drawn and the front of her dress was damp from the dripping water.

Finally, she looked over at Jacob and snapped "You could get me an apron or something instead of standing there."

He hung his head, shook his head. "I'm sorry, Mabel I was wondering how long it would take for you to ask."

She sighed and nodded. "Okay. I'm a little out of practice."

Did he pick up on her lack of kitchen dish washing prowess or the way she talked all English like – she could not be sure. In a few minutes, he'd returned to the kitchen with an apron in tow. It was plain, no pacific tidepool blue like in the entryway of her New York apartment. It smelled musty.

"Sorry about the smell. Was up in the attic. It belonged to my Mother."

She'd heard that about the Amish, how they saved and reused everything as much as possible. She smiled, held out her hands, but he shook his head. He motioned for her to turn around.

She laughed a little and turned away from him. He slipped the apron over her neck and draped the cloth over her front. He pulled the strings together and tied them behind her.

She looked down at the apron. It was two sizes too large. It was the color of heritage cream.

She turned around to face him. "Thank you, Jacob. This will do quite nicely."

He nodded. "Good. I'm glad you can make use of it. Now I must go tend to the fields."

"When can I expect you?" She turned and resumed washing the dishes.

"A bit later this afternoon. Would a later lunch be agreeable?"

"Of course."

What else could she do, but agree. What else could she think of except was she safe here in Jacob's house of mercurial artic gray.

Would he understand or even accept her English life of color, her fondness for material things, her designer life, her ability to pick the right color paint for the right room. Could he accept her one failure where she'd gotten the room colors of the high-rise condo all right, but read the owner all wrong? He had meant to jump, she was sure. Anyone who knew him and heard their argument would say she pushed him. Jacob was safe with her, for her that much she knew.

"We'll see you when I get back. I'll wash up first."

She said nothing to this only looking over her shoulder and giving him a soft smile.

It was late afternoon when she saw him again. He was lugging two buckets of water. One he set by the sink. The other he poured into a wash basin.

She had the kitchen swept, and their lunch simmering on the stove. She had cooked a stew with veggies and potatoes. She had attempted to make a cake she kept eyeing in the oven.

He sniffed the air and walked back into the kitchen. "Smells very good. I'm going to wash up before we eat."

They ate in silence. He helped her clean the

kitchen in silence.

After the kitchen was clean, they each retired to their rooms. She slept sound she realized not waking up until the sun shone through the windows filling the plain room with an antiguan daybreak yellow.

Their routine went on like that for a few weeks, then months. Soon everyone in the community figured out they weren't related.

It was maybe after their barn raising and the planting of trees. She told him she wanted shaded cedar – beautiful green trees to line the walkway off the two-story small white house with an outbuilding and field.

The barn was to be used for a horse or two and a mule, to store farm equipment and maybe crops they planned to grow and harvest.

Together they painted it and the three bedrooms of the old house an equestrian hazel even though color, even tan, was frowned upon – everything should be plain white inside or so she was told. At night, they'd sit and swing on the front porch swing and sip lemonade. He gave her lessons in how to be Amish.

Six months in, she seemed to be getting the hang of it all when he surprised her again. They'd shared little more than hugs and kisses on the cheek. He came up behind her and pulled her close to him whispering in her ear.

"There's talk of you being English. There's talk of why we aren't married."

She turned to him and placed her arms on his. "Then we must stop this talk."

He stared at her with his ocean blue eyes. "You are really English, aren't you?"

She nodded. His hands dropped to his sides.

"Do you want to share with me how you came to be here?"

She nodded again. "After supper, we will talk."

He took his breakfast plate of sausage, biscuits, gravy, eggs, and bacon from her and sat at the table. She fixed another plate with smaller quantities and joined him.

They ate in silence. As soon as he was done, he let out a long burb. He grinned and hid his head.

She giggled. "You have a very good appetite."

She kept busy the rest of the day cleaning the dishes, preparing lunch and later on supper, changing sheets on the beds, doing the wash, and sweeping. The day folded into evening much quicker than she thought. The days in Pennsylvania melted into one another fast not slow. In her old English life, she was in a constant busy state.

She no longer missed it. The apartment, the clothes, the nightclubs, the parties, the everything. It seemed worlds away – the need to be seen, to be seen wearing the right clothing designer, the need to be seen on the arm of the right person at the perfect time. She had been climbing the ranks a little too fast – too much attention from too many married higher ups.

The one that mentored her the most ended up dead and she was the last one to see him alive. She'd been doing lines with him, of course, and had to leave for an early meeting the next morning an impromptu housing commercial where she was paid $1400 for an hour of work reciting a few lines about the newest must have apartment in New York City. She'd lucked into the business easy enough emailing a resume to a rather well-known designer looking for a few interns for a renovation project near her hometown on the coast of South Carolina. She'd moved after that and did drawings including designing spectacular parties for hire to keep her pocket money flowing.

She wasn't a household designer but her reputation, her name, her face could be found in a quick internet search. She mouthed the word "Mabel" to herself. She whispered again "I am Mabel."

"Mabel?"

She sat up in surprise. Jacob stood behind her. He held soap, a washcloth and a tub of water. She looked at him.

He smiled and asked in a quiet voice. "May I?"

She nodded. Jumped a little as he touched her with the washcloth.

His hands were shaking as he glided the cool cloth up and down around her neck, arms and shoulders.

"You've never been with a woman, have you?" she whispered.

He shook his head. "I'm the confirmed bachelor here. But I don't want to be. I like the company you've given me."

She turned around in full view of him. He dropped his head, his chin, his eyes.

"It's okay. You can look."

She reached out, touched his face and lifted it until his eyes met hers.

"The things I've done, Jacob. The things I've been accused of--."

"None of that matters."

He pulled her towards him and kissed her – not his first kiss, but only his second he later told her the night before they were to be married.

The wedding was planned and commenced in a hurry – most of the community wanted it done to ease the talk of their living together "in sin." Their days went by fast with him in the fields and her keeping house.

She forgot about being English. She had forgotten how to be English.

A year passed and then another. It was Fall again, almost two years since she'd disappeared from the English world. The simplest of things can cause an avalanche a thought that ran through her head at the curt nod of recognition from the tourist (a woman, her former apartment neighbor) climbing off one of the Amish Buggy rides. Her name was Anna, that much she remembered. Her accent was thick New York, her hair dark, short and her skin pale.

She shouted across the parking lot "Roz. Roz! My oh my you're in a heap of trouble. I got your mail, stacked it up in my apartment – in a box now, there's so much of it."

Roz now Mabel looked away. She had been looking in the train gift shop of the Caboose Motel looking for something for Jacob's birthday. The buggy driver, Samuel, hopped off – he walked over to where the two women stood facing one another.

He spat on the ground and cackled. "Why you must be mistaken. This is Mabel Lapp married to Jacob Lapp – they were meant to be together the first time they saw each other. Of course, it was arranged."

The woman, Anna, pursed her lips, crossed her arms, and scowled. "Roz? Pre-arranged marriage? No way. Not her. She was a spit fire if I've ever seen one. Always in some kind of trouble even if she was a good Designer." She shook her head. "I'm so sorry, Mrs. Lapp – thinking you were that no count charlatan."

"No trouble at all, Miss--?"

"Anna. Anna Langston."

"I'm sorry to have upset you."

Anna brushed off her shorts and black tee. "No

problem at all. It was silly of me to think you, a gentle kind Amish woman, could have been her, that Roz." She laughed, cackled, her head reeled back and she giggled some more. "What was I thinking? I'm going to head back to my room now. Sorry for the confusion."

With that one encounter, she remained Amish – no one ever questioned it again.

One night she questioned herself. She sat on the front porch waiting for Jacob. She swung back and forth on the swing swigging lemonade between swings.

Did she miss it? Did she miss TV, movies and the news, designer clothes and fancy restaurants? Here her life was daily and every day – days of growing food, shopping, community and church socials which were held in different farm houses as there weren't any actual churches and sleeping with her husband, legal marriage or not, they had all embraced her because of him.

Roz now Mabel watched her husband from the window. The sunset was a perfect blend of orange and yellow.

She had turned her back on the English world – escaped – her fate there, had she stayed, would've meant lawsuits, maybe prison. Now she prayed, sewed and mended clothes, washed by hand, spent most of her days cooking and cleaning in the dim gray glow.

She'd left the dark of white, black and grey for a world full of colors – a rainbow of choices, her new life ahead.

Ken Weene

Of prayers and rhymes

A gray brown dove took residence beside our stairs.
Settling with one last wings' flutter, she
had taken final wounded refuge there.
Then, stirring from time to time
with stricken coos, she made it clear
that her demise was coming near.
I saw her stir from time to time
and wondered if I might give her quick release
or by chanting prayers and happy rhymes
I could perchance relieve her tremored fears.
Instead, I stood above and mimed
my sad farewell and kissed the desert air.
In the end, mortality took her soul away
and left her down and feathered body for decay.

Keith E. Sparks Jr.

In Loving Memory

I can not find the will to sleep.

To dream to life a phantom fear
that lingers there in haunted depths.
Where ripples blur archaic runes
the talons carve behind closed eyes
that halt the rhythm, breaking time,
where echoes sound in empty rooms
that bear the scars of each new death
which springs to life when sleep is near.

I can not find the will to sleep.

The Stars Fade, But Not Those Eyes…

I've made my wish upon a broken star
and rattled fractured bells that won't ring true
in hopes the frantic music hides the scars
the way that darkened shadows often do.

As Faltering, The lights that paint the sky
collapse from their positions in the night.
To offer us a momentary lie
while wishing what we will and what we might

we watch the flashing streak that fades away—
The way that burning embers often do—
and pray that all the wishes that we've made
will somehow find a way to all come true…

The way they often do within your eyes
where every wish I've made is realized…

The Poetic Heart

We lay the heart of passion on a page
And bring to life the subtle shapes of love
In gentle folds emotions can engage
That lead us to the dreams we're dreaming of

Where paper crafted hearts become the norm
In flowing scripts that bear a lover's name
As each precision crease we make transforms
To tintinnabulation Unrestrained

Where every hope we have we pray remains
To keep from falling crumpled to the floor
Where fragile folded hearts are often slain
And trampled under feet for longing for

The love for which each tender heart was made
With gentle hands and paper cuts in spades...

Lisa White

Understanding.

I suppose we were the tides

And the phases of the moon.

Ebbing and flowing.

Waxing and waning.

Coming on full and strong

Then suddenly disappearing

And without waves.

No words, no explanations

Just an understanding of how it should be.

Energies.

Love is not lost, its merely regifted
just as seeds of flowers in winters snow
come again in spring when deaths grip is lifted
it is natures way, of letting us know

that people we love, never truly leave
they bloom in others we meet on the way
and unto all the memories we cleave
we find, all the ways in which, they still stay

in friendships we form with such gentle ease
the love and kindness we see in their eyes
or the warmth of their hugs like summers breeze
coming from the bluest of pure blue skies

and within our grief, we find deeper hope
of more beautiful ways, in which to cope.

Maggie Mackay

Seanchaidh

Imagine this steward of a land's history,
its stories, words, on a winter's evening
wind howling, Strathnaver folk cooried-in, ready.

This master of memory, acrobat with rhythm,
plays with repeated sounds: 'the dragon drew fire'
'a moon hung above the mist'
like a musician strumming chords on strings.

What can you call him but
keeper of old lore, all by heart,
from the heart to the community's heart,

a continuum of voices recording
laws, ancestry, ballads, sagas, songs
for all time in regular beats and repeats.

Takotsubo Cardiomyopathy

He'd gone. Overnight.
Never to return.
Short breath, chest pain find me.
An echo cardiogram probes
balloons and bulges.
My left ventricle shapeshifts
into an octopus trap for now,
pot narrow at the neck,
rounded at the bottom.
I'm trapped, sore, aching.
Time seals the chambers with kintsugi,
part of the history of my pain.

Dorthy LaVern Spencer McCarthy

An Old Man's Wallet

His wallet holds the scraps of yesterday
with faded photos dearest to his heart;
A raffle ticket, notice of a play
attended when his daughter had a part;
A stub from some wild party in the rain
at college when he went where laughter led;
A tiny rosebud wrapped in cellophane
from his true love's bouquet when they were wed;
A snip of ribbon done in earthy tones
from some dead soldier's grave across the sea;
Such pieces of his life are all he owns,
each remnant bringing back a memory.

These treasures, and a letter from a friend
will hold his world together till the end.

A Rose In Heaven

I visit Mother's grave this time of year,
intent on clearing moss and weeds away.
Red roses there evoke a happy tear,
for I remember scenes, a summer day--
the garden where she tended blooms of light,
the same as I transplanted, still aglow
beside her stone, that angels, lost at night,
might find her resting place while ages go.
No other flowers ever brought a smile,
but red, red roses made her spirit fly.
My mother loved their simple grace and style,
and now that she resides with God on high
I hope that somewhere in eternity
she wears one in her hair and thinks of me.

Andrew Scott

Laying Here

Barely remember how I got here,
laying scared in this hospital bed.

Do remember talking to my wife,
telling her about the shortness of breath
and the heart that was about to burst.
Thinking it was biking in the heat.

Do remember the fear in her voice
and the look on her face
when she came to get me
to take me to this bed.
I felt her tears.

Do remember them taking blood,
placing all the wires
and monitors on me
without saying why.

Do remember thinking
this was how my mother passed.
That memory racing through
my constant working mind.

Do not remember what
the doctor said to me
about the rapid beats
in my frail heart.

All I truly remember
is laying here in fear.

Johanne Lee

The tapping stick

The top hatted man is well buttoned
and totally upstanding, carrying staunch support,
marking the road
in tapping sounds—
Make way—
Stand back –
As the lady crosses herself

That's kind, I think
I wonder if she blesses herself feared of deaths claws
or to praise the dead
as cars block the other side, impatiently
not knowing the dead or that these minutes count…

I hold myself in tear strained tissues and wish I could
hide
from noticing the flowers that sit complimenting the
grain...

Solid.. I think..

Will last year's same as her, I didn't want to see death

twice
so had artificial flowers- tulips—locally sourced
not travelled from Amsterdam

Tears fall knowing we won't sing that spring again
The thought is there

He's stopped now..
still buttoned solemn
stock still—
head bowed—

I see another driver undecided on etiquette and I think..
Wait—
I even say please
Today is stiff upper lipped and snotty tissues
never mind work- the shopping
whatever it is you think you need

She crosses herself as we pass
so, she's not all bad
and the well buttoned man gets in the car
He has walked enough—same as her
I might remember his countenance
his polite walk
maybe his tapping stick

But I'll remember everything about her...

Michael Minassian

My Grandfather Suffers A Fatal Heart Attack

After Climbing Three Flights of Stairs

When I arrived
at my grandparent's apartment
in the Bronx, my grandmother
cried when she saw me.

She told me they had come home
from a party when my grandfather
slumped on the couch—
He never woke up, she said.

I wandered into their bedroom
and saw his watch on the nightstand—
next to the watch was a water glass
with his false teeth inside.

The EMTs had removed his dentures
and handed them to my grandmother—
I imagined they spoke to her

as she placed them in the glass.

I could hear words
gurgling underwater—
how could he be dead,
and his teeth still speak to me?

I listened to his voice tell me
how far he had traveled
from Armenia to America,
leaving behind the unmarked graves

of his parents, first wife, and child,
and the songs the dead still sing,
if you listened closely,
if you remembered them at all.

* Originally appeared in *HyeBred Magazine* 2021.

Victor Schwartzman

Andrea And Her Body

From her earliest days, Andrea took her body for granted.

Andrea became pregnant and her body changed. Her baby forced her to listen to it, but her daughter was born and after she stopped breast feeding her relationship with her body returned to normal.

In her thirties Andrea continued to do what she did in her twenties. Her body felt great. In her forties, she began wearing loose clothing and she started to lose stamina and noticed sagging where she had been firm. In her fifties, her hair began to gray and one day in her mid-sixties, Andrea tried to get up from a chair and could not--until she gripped the chair's arms and pushed herself up. "Okay, I've heard you," Andrea muttered to her body as she sat in a chair and put on her new reading glasses.

"Have you?" she heard a deep voice ask.

She looked around the room but no one was there. Andrea shrugged the experience off and forgot about it. More years went by. One day, Andrea sat in her chair feeling old. She muttered, "My body and I have to talk."

"Finally," a deep voice replied. "We're 73."

Andrea sat up, startled. She realized the voice was her body. "You're talking to me!" she said to herself. "But why now?"

"Honey, I talked plenty. Remember getting out of breath on the stairs? Our arteries and veins are full of sludge, our muscles flab. It's too late."

"It is never too late!" Mortality stared her in the face. For years she tried medications but the side effects became too great.

At 81, Andrea sat reflecting. "I've screwed up," she mumbled.

"You sure have," the deep voice replied, exasperated. "We're a mess. I'd hoped for an end clean and fast. A heart attack. Now, who knows?"

"I know you expected more of me." "Nope. Knew early on. But I always hoped to avoid this type of humiliation."

Andrea pushed herself up from the chair. "So, we're going to die?"

"Soon?"

"It's always too soon."

"What should we do?" she asked. "A walk would be good," her body hopefully replied. And they went outside for a walk.

You now choose how this story ends:

One: I start walking, then decide to go for it and jog. I don't listen to my body and keep jogging until I die from a massive heart attack.

Two: After the walk, I go to my doctors. Pills are the solution. They put me on an experimental drug trial. The medication has side effects and I die from a massive heart attack.

Three: After years of neglect, I finally start listening to my body. Our last years together are remarkably pleasant. I learn to listen and accept limitations.

Four: This whole listening to your body thing pisses me off! I enter a cryogenic facility and am frozen.

Sometime in the future, I will get a new body which will do whatever I want. After two weeks of being frozen, however, there is a power outage and I melt.

Manuela Palacios

Heart Matters (Haibun)

Iambic is
the prosody of the heart —
blood pumped in verse.

Let's have, my love, a heart-to-heart talk about the labyrinth garden we have planted through our years together. Its location may not be practical —we simply followed our hearts— but its paths have guided us in the intricate journey through life.

I'll pour my heart out and admit I haven't always believed our garden would prosper: the neighbouring forest casting its perennial shade, the unruly soil, the indefatigable moles… but we had our hearts set on it and there it is, a healing haven.

Four cardiac chambers:
each a congenial stanza
for the transient guest.

We've heard of other labyrinths built into the floors of churches to offer a meditative itinerary to those with their heart in the right place —a substitute for pilgrimage routes, some say.

But going to the heart of the matter, my love, we will also find labyrinth gardens in hospitals and other oases for the cure of mind and body. On meandering along their paths, breathing slows down, the mind relaxes and blood pressure relieves our hearts, but no fear, this won't make us half-hearted!

Enjambement makes
blood flow in run-on lines
to lungs and cells.

Melissa Mulvihill

The Elephants Only I Can See

I pay attention to the darkness in my breathing by focusing on the elephants only I can see.

When I say "pay," I mean full cash payment up front, like the time my husband just wanted to cut up an avocado for lunch, and instead drilled a serrated knife into the base of his index finger. He left his payment on the kitchen floor and the countertop. He even sacrificed some nerves.

When I say "attention," I mean the scrape of the catheter that was threaded up my groin on a mission to burn misbehaving cardiac cells. I mean the tone of my unsedated voice ricocheting around the electrophysiology lab, bouncing off the computer screens, *it burns*. What I really meant was *you're burning me*, so, when I say "attention," you know, I mean, the wave of fentanyl that came way too late.

When I say "darkness," I mean the ledge outside of Ansel's Cave, where at night I hear packs of coyotes dispatching their prey by ripping into it on the Sharon conglomerate. Their echoing howls run slick, right down through the rocks, right down through the mossy pebbles, right down to the roots of the ginormous tree that everyone just knew was going to fall, that everyone felt could not withstand one more Lake Erie blow. *That thing's gonna have to come down,* everyone said, *or it'll be in the way of everything when it falls.* They said *falls* but I know they meant *fails*. That's what everyone means when they talk about things in imminent danger of falling.

When I say "breathing," I mean the release of desperate puffs of regret, in that tone of voice someone uses when they're about to break me apart and they know it, but they do it anyway. I mean the mocking scream of adrenaline oozing towards my extremities digging deep into my limbic system, prying me out of the bed, begging me to *do something, fight or flee, but don't just lie there and sweat and gasp.*

When I say "focus," I mean that day I was walking up Pioneer Bridle Trail and I saw an old woman on the trail with her blind dog and she said to her little dog, *don't call me an old woman*. As I passed by, she said, *I can walk to the moon and back because I still have great legs*. I nodded, while she hunkered over the little blind dog, leading him by his heart, in teeny looping circles all around the trail.

When I say "elephants," I mean that through my greyish

astigmatism, through my old farsightedness, through the back glow of the villages of Burton and Middlefield to the northeast, our trees break in such interesting ways, looking like a failed sympathetic nervous system or elephants. That matriarch right there, stands guard over me, her vast back flank leading the way, the rest of her herd following along behind her, around the perimeter of the distant easement.

When I say, "only," I mean that the matriarch will pin all of my poachers, with the precision of a gladiator, one tremendous knee crushing their backs, one tusk, one jab, one last, deep thrust for grievances past.

When I say "see," I mean the resentment in the chambers of my heart, where I shove blood artlessly between grief and tornados, like the one that uprooted the biggest, strongest tree in our woods, when it was just minding its own damn business.

Calan McCarthy

Mennonite Mile

THE TIMBER HUT was candlelit and sparse within and when he moved from the desk the flames pitched and leaned then righted themselves. That night the wind moaned in the stovepipe while lightning flared in the north and no rain came until firstlight. The breach in the door intruded squally from without and leavened the embers in the firehole to lurch and strain and he bridled the crack with a buffalo pelt his father had slain the year eighteen and ninety. He watched the flame of the candle for a time and the wax pool on to the oak surface and the stern portraits of his forebears looked out from the lumber facade on to that solitary room and as he fixed on their faces he considered what form of reasoning shifted through their minds at the moment of rendering.

Out on that terra damnata before dusk he had stood and qualified the vast ocean from the bluff and the waves drew brutal kerfs of white spume as they rolled inland with impunity and the pumice wind gnawed at the bone and skin like rangy death rodents and the steel sun fused through the cloudsprent sky while tiny sanderlings skittered along the brackish shoreline. A gibbous moon hung high in that void and he knew a storm was coming.

He rose from the desk and laboured toward the door moved the pelt aside with his boot then opened the door. A revolt of wind snuffed the candles out then cuffed him as he stepped outside. He waded out yonder toward the fell and steadied himself against the stone coping took the pail and set it down into the well, hauled it up then took it inside. The only light now within was firelight so he tendered a flame to the candles with a brand from the fire. He took the gourd from the bucket and filled the brass kettle with water then set it firm in the flames. He sat studying the embers. That morning he had buried the corpse of his father out in the scrubland. Took him above two hours to dig that grave and the wind was swelling even then. A lone buzzard hovered aloft watching like some stubborn cloud then dove in for forage as soon as his back was turned. The day before he had fashioned a coffin from remnants of timber, lay his father in his best suit then sealed the lid shut and that same night was spent in morbid wake in the silence of death's presence and he irked to recall some scriptural verse to quiet his mind which had been learned by rote some years before.

Nothing came.

Humble words of eulogy were tendered at the

foot of that grave and a grey wolf watched on from a crag aloft while he gathered and set about a formation of stones for a cairn to chronicle the burial. With his father in the earth and the wind howling at the door he felt the outset of loneliness take hold and as he stared into the flames he drew solemn on his tobacco and set his mind at prior days of mirth.

HE WAS SECOND BORN of four and in him a soul prevising to liberate itself. He came into this world amid the heat and grit of alien territory where his folk had settled among Mennonite. Born to colony life. Roots he would drug up in adolescence and leave behind for good. The Missouri River his home. His folk sworn to refuse both social and military service. Forbidden fruit he would later sample.

The gebet dominated the day after he had laboured the fields and livestock and the minister led the congregation on to some deific plain with pious hymn and sacred augury of men now lost, and through his laconic sermon he aimed to attest the meaning and purpose of their lives into sharp focus as they kneeled reverently with bowed head before God. And as the child watched on in question his mind strayed to a world beyond the doctrines of the elders and boundaries of the colony.

The farm was upriver and forty-five mile north a dam and spillway had been built on the James River and it was knowledge of this that taunted the boy. His day commenced in the blazing heat and at nine years of age he was sent to a neighbouring farm to help break the virgin prairie frontier. He rode out on to the brush after communal breakfast and ministered prayer and passed the chapel and school where ancient verse and strange tongue emulated. He stood his horse a while to regard his father and brother grind wheat into flour in that structure of white pestle while the hatches waded and moiled and his mother and sisters waved on from their chores. In the trace his horse threw a shoe and farmer Irwin took time out of his day to teach the boy proper farriering and with the hoofpick the boy cleaned out debris from the underside of the hoof then tested the nails in the shoe before hammering it on. Irwin fit the shoe to the hoof and let Jacob tap the nails into former holes. He showed him the use of the cinchblock to tighten the shoe to hoof and pry the nail with nippers and crook the heads with a clincher and they repeated the process until it had branded finite in his mind.

His day was long in that sultry sun where man and beast were pushed beyond their limits hoeing down with a team of horses and their walkingplows in tow, and his wages were scant and he begrudged turning his laboured cent over to the colony and returning there after his absence. On that day and many following he spent the night at the farm and lay out in the night sky watching the Pleiades arc the empty black void with the moon burning some great white hole of coruscation and earlier he joined the fieldhands in forging some towering bonfire with the midden and they sat and regarded the flames spitting and lurching like some tormented viper with its splinters lofting up into the darkness. They warmed their mess on the embers and Kinter took to regaling a tune on the fiddle while they ate and drank and smoked and Jacob squailed at the pyre with loose stobs and the coyotes related with their yammering. When morning came their heads were bedevilled and sotol bitten yet their day commenced as before and they hove forth on to that parched environ drudging their way through the hours of heat and mud and sweat.

When he rode in one evening after his labour the boy Jude had preceded him in the stable. He had not seen him on first entering for his mind was fixed on dismounting and uncinching the horse and just as he was about to stand in his stirrup he felt a harsh jerk on the back of his shirt which was ripped in two as he hit the ground. The horse shied and scuffed with the boy's left foot mired still in the stirrup and had the trailing reins snagged about his left arm.

Best you be stayin put in that there dirt, Jude said, else I be kickin you down with my boot.

Jacob lifted his face from the loam and regarded him with animus.

What in hell ye do that for?

Do I gotta have reason?

With me ye has. Dont care who ye pa is.

Jude was the son of the elder Hofer and was burly in frame and manner with a broad scar lashed across his chin which he'd acquired from the buckle of his father's belt for cussing and spitting in his face.

My pa says you aint fit to be part a this here colony on account a you bein stray in the head.

What?

You heard. Stray in the head. That mean somethin aint workin right upstairs.

I know what it mean asshat.

The contempt in his face was malign and berate and he sat up unwound the reins from his arm picked himself up off the floor and brushed down his trousers. He took hold of the reins and tied them to the hitching rail then swung round with his right arm outstretched and whacked Jude's cheekbone hard with his balled fist. Jude dropped to the ground with a thud and he was rolling about like some trammelled pig squealing and yipping with both hands pressed to his face with his knees bent up toward his chest.

You'll pay for that, he said as he rose from the dust and within a split second he had propelled himself forward and hauled his heavy frame at Jacob and they both hit the ground like some weighted gunny of grain. Jacob gasped violently and was winded and he lay there for a few moments watching the dust settle as he drew breath. Jude had rebound off him and was lain face down in the arid mud choking and whooping and by and by Jacob hove up and was lurching toward him then threw himself headlong at Jude's limbs where for a time they slogged and grappled and Jacob pinned him to the floor as he commenced to shove handfuls of dirt into his mouth. A cloud of dust was pensile amid thrashing limbs and malicious yammering and barking as the ruckus commenced and before long Jacob's father entered the stable to separate the two boys from the contention.

What in hell is goin on here?

But Jacob was still trying to get at Jude and it was all Joseph could do to hold his son back for he was slugging about like some halfbroken colt with his face hot and ferric and his gaze morose.

I said whats all this then? Is you two fixin to get yerselves flogged or somethin? Yous know you caint behave in this here manner. Why some curious punishment will incur an you know it.

Please dont be tellin my pa nothin sir. I caint be takin no further beatin.

Now Jude I aint sayin Im goin to them elders just yet but what I is suggestin is that we rectify this here matter right here and now between three of us. Otherwise I be forced to take it to your pa understood? Now whats gone on? Jacob?

He done pull me from my horse soon as I come in here and fore I can even hitch off the saddle then he took to callin me names sir. Said I was stray in the head.

Did he now. An what you got to say bout this here accusation Jude? You done this? You pull him clean off his horse unawares?

Jude was sniffling and bawling by this point and he was stood with one shoe discalced since it had dislodged itself in the fray. Yessir, he said. Aint meanin nothin by it. Thems the truth. I just repeatin what my pa done said is all.

Well Im sure your pa aint meanin for you to set upon no one on their horse now is he? Im thinkin that there's your idea. I right?

Yessir.

Furthermore your pa should know better than to be inventin tall tales bout folk here in the colony. True or not. That done make him no betteren some churlish adolescent himself. What you fixin to say bout that? You think he be settin good example? Christian like?

No sir.

No sir he aint. Now Jude, I seen you apply that there irritation a yours on more than three occasion an Im guessin your pa either aint seen it or he be turnin a blind eye to it an you know it aint right to be tormentin them thats younger an you. Nor any folk for that matter. So what you say we settle this here scrap by yous apologisin to Jacob? But Im wantin some straight leanin oath from you indicatin yous gone halt that there hectorin. Else I be havin words with your pa. Ye hear?

Yessir. Sorry sir.

Not to me damn it. Hims who you been takin issue with. Well go on.

Sorry Jacob.

And.

I swears I wont be provokin no other a no kind from this here day.

Right then. Now y'all shake hands an be done with it.

The boys shook hands but with a measure of loathness on Jacob's part then Jude stood and stared at the ground.

Next time I sees you baitin them there bairn you is fixin to have some mighty reckonin. An not just from me. An I get to feelin you aint much enchanted with the idea a your pa payin his wrath neither. So best you pay heed boy cause I aint the sort to go back on my word. Now you go on then.

Yessir.

And that boy Jude scanned his inordinate gaze across the dirt to seek out his shoe and he slunk forth with the impact of some idle sloth picked up his shoe turned back to regard Joseph shamefaced and cowed then sauntered out into the yard. Jacob was mute and walked over to his horse to uncinch the saddle and as he loosened the girthstraps his torn shirt parted and raw scars were visible in their nefarious state of aggravation. His father measured the roiled facet jarred and uneasy and he took his son by the arm to face him then held him by the shoulders with both hands. Jacob could no more than look him straight in the eye so he stared down at his father's worn shoes.

Who done this to you boy?

He gave no answer.

Look at me son. Who done this?

Jacob stared into the black of his father's eyes and he bore down a whole spate of emotion and it circumscribed about him with such retribution he could not utter a word.

You know you can tell me any damn thing. I aint gone punish you none.

There was a heavy silence. The horse whinnied.

Was it one a them fieldhands at Irwins farm?

The boy nodded it wasn't.

Them lashes look fresh as primed meat son an Im thinkin that there violence can only be inflicted by one other individual. An it aint your kin.

The boy was at essay with himself to preserve his silence then he could feel his eyes filling up and the tears emerged and made a trace down one side of his mud peppered face.

His father qualified the wounds with circumspection and a storm was foraging across his every feature with the ferocity of some nebulous spectre and he dropped down to one knee to address his son with absolute amenity.

Now you dont have to say nothin. You just nod ye hear?

The boy nodded in agreement.

Now Im guessin he give you some coal black warnin not to say nothin. I right?

Jacob nodded.

Judgin by them scars look like some a them aint so fresh as others. How long this here been goin on boy? Weeks?

He nodded no.

Months?

He nodded and began to weep.

That son of a bitch. Now I know clear as shit it were Baurock but you never spoke nothin to me bout who the culprit were ye hear? You aint said a word. An you dont need to of neither. An that alright. I might be slow as a turtle some but what I aint is stupid.

What you gone do Pa? If he find out I done told you he gone kill me.

No. You aint told me nothin son. You never utter his name. Dont you worry none. I gone see to it he caint set on his haunches for week.

Joseph rose from his knee and set out across the yard with asperity branded athwart his face and he charged towards the house in a fit of mania and tore through the chicken coop like some malefic cyclone and the fowl strew their plumage and evicted their stations in a throe of panic as he commenced forth toward the adobe hut and Jacob was hollering after him like some goading drover beset by an impending crag and he could no more stop him than any man can the unruly tide. Jacob's mother was now stood in the doorway regarding the commotion with question and she was calling out to attain reason while her offspring convoked and glared in bewilderment yet no account was cited and deaf to it all Joseph took up the rifle and shucked it back and the spent shells discharged to the ground then he levered in a fresh round and sallied out toward the hearth of Baurock propulsive in enterprise. By this point the colony citizens were eluded by the logic of the business and were trailing behind him like he was the Hamelin gambit himself and they were alarmed by the sight of the firearm since any such munitions were prohibited and usurped due to settlement rule.

He approached the portico at the front of the property and hove up the steps to the door and with the butt of the rifle forced entry without so much as a knock and as he cocked the rifle Baurock was stood rigid and aghast scripture in hand and Joseph measured him feralwise with his gaze and he launched forth charging Baurock rearward into a corner and Baurock in his paltry state stepped back and had his spine pressed to the wall then recoiled his tall frame to the floorboards his hands uplifted to fend off the revenant before him. What in God's name has possessed you to this fiendish state? Baurock said in his temporal air of grievance. Am I not brethren to you? Tell me instantly what it is I have done in offense. For God is my witness I've done naught to smite the Joseph Stahl.

Joseph glared baleful at the minister and sweat was beading at his forehead and a motley of acolyte faces peered in through the windows without as they awaited some inimical explication. He aimed the barrel of the rifle at Baurock's head and exhaled deeply through his nose and qualified him with halberd eye then said, I gone ask you one time to bring that there quirt a yours you so attach to so as all folk here can survey the piece for emselves.

Baurock was mute.

Joseph raised the rifle and fired up into the scantling and the explosion clove sherds of wood which fell upon the boards like pinnate and the crowd jounced and gasped with harrowed faces then he deployed the rifle back at Baurock's head.

You git, he said, else I gone shoot somethin you caint be without.

Robin Holmes

HEARTFELT

Embedded below my rib cage,
a thumping, throbbing underground station,
where blood is squeezed and squashed
into arterial carriages, stops at all vital organs,
lungs, kidneys, liver, brain, St Pancreas.
Red line, *Central,* travelling from brain to toe,
Blue line, returning veins, *District or Circle,*
services almost every second, with
ventricles, valves, chambers, aorta,
all pumping and purring, as smoothly
as a Rolls Royce Silver Cloud.

and though held in marvel and awe,

hearts decay and age. Substances and stress

erode efficiency, lines become blocked

with the leaves of cholesterol,

boulder clots derail, sometimes fatally.

The heart's pendulum loses precision,

arrhythmias arrive, the heart stutters.

Surgeons, like plumbers, hover

with a bulging tool box;

pacemakers, valves, stents,

ingenious space age technologies,

the heart being more mapped than the moon.

Yet the heart exists, as poets know it,

and often show it, within a mysterious ether;

call it persona, psyche, soul or spirit.

Hearts can be broken ,

and sometimes mend.

The heart is a lonely hunter,

everybody has a hungry heart.

Wordsworth's heart leapt at the sight of a rainbow,

Dylan, deserted, felt a cork screwed on his heart.

Grief and sorrow pierce the heart like briars,

separation and divorce wrap the heart in barbed wire.

All euphemisms belie, that

the heart of the matter is,

the heart is more, so much more

than matter.

Sinead Coxhill

Stillness

"You have to be prepared to lose this child"
the midwife's words assaulted my ears
assaulted my whole body
two of them stayed by my side
holding my hands, murmuring to me
kind words I couldn't take in

a few hours later into my labour
a junior doctor arriving
"An injection might be the answer"
I clung to his words
as to a life raft
everything might still work out
he left the room but didn't return

the frustrations of the midwives
as my contractions grew closer together
eventually he returned with the syringe
which he passed over   and left

my legs were clamped together
in fear   dread of this birth
which spelt death

hope the doctor had ushered in
now ebbed away
as I imagined that little life would

soon it was over

his lifeless body
placed in my arms
he was beautiful
but his bruised skin
told of a painful journey
in   and   out   of this world

Yvonne Hamilton

The Last Dance

She put the phone down, moved the box of crackers, eased herself carefully into her rocking chair and gazed at her husband, her mind drifting back over the years – back to the first time she saw him.

She had shared a flat near the university with three others. All busy with lectures on various courses during the week but ready to party on Saturday nights. She remembered the hectic preparation for the Hops in the Students' Union: the piles of dresses that accumulated on the beds as they were considered and rejected; the rush for the iron before someone else got it; the piles of makeup scattered on all the surfaces in the bedroom; the queue at the bathroom; the swapping of petticoats; the borrowing of shoes. All this accompanied by the drone of hair dryers in the building excitement as hair was back combed and sprayed firmly in place before the short walk to the union.

It was a mysterious place: – dim-lit, smoke-filled, packed with bodies shouting above the rhythmic thump of the music that vibrated though the floor into the dancing feet; the centre of the floor always filled with open necked shirts and swirling petticoats; the walls hidden by the crowds waiting to be asked or waiting to ask.

That night they pushed their way to their usual meeting place – a place to which they returned between dances, a place where they appeared to belong if no-one asked them to dance. It was important not to look alone, un-wanted. She had returned from two dances, both with regulars, friends from her course, who danced with her every week, when she saw him standing between two chatting groups. He was looking at her and she knew, she knew that he would ask her to dance. She knew, she knew that she would accept.

He held her hand as they threaded their way to join the heaving mass of bodies and held her close as they moved to the music. She thought he must surely hear the frantic beating of her heart through her cheek pressed close to his shoulder or the hand he held close to his chest At the end of the Section he thanked her before she returned to her group. She remembered thinking, *'please come back before someone else asks'*. He did, as she knew he would and stayed with her for the last dance. The last dance was the important one. Someone might ask to walk you home.

As the final note faded away he put his arm round her shoulder and said "I'd like to walk you home." She hoped that the bolt of pure joy that shot through her was hidden behind the smile that lit up her face as she said, "I'd like that too."

The chat on the way was easy – her course, his sport, her family, his home – till they stopped in the small patch of shadow between two streetlights close to the flat. He turned to face her, took her face between his hands and kissed her. A sweet, gentle questioning kiss. A kiss that asked *are you alright, is this alright,* a kiss that lit up her whole being and took her breath away.

He stepped back, hands on her shoulder, to look at her. "Now" he said "Am I going to see you again Elizabeth Brown?" Her heart soared with happiness.

Yes. She had always known he was different, right from that first look on that first night – wonderfully, magically, excitingly different for all these years.

The sound of the doorbell brought her back. She struggled up and headed to the door stroking him gently on the cheek as she went. They burst in with their bags, their badges, their uniforms, stamping the snow off their feet and brushing against the Christmas tree so that the decorations jangled. She shut the door against the flashing lights.

"I phoned" she said. "He's in the sitting room."

It's too late" she whispered.

Mary Farrell

hearth matters

the Cottage snivelled

as it remembered

there had been trilling laughs and dancing feet, the swirls and curls of toddlers tumbling
smells of yeast and crusts, savouries and sweet crumbles, beer a-hopping and mint-sharp teas
just-birthed lambs, crook-eared sheepdogs, ancient cats curled tight on the hearthstones
with love flowing tween souls sealed by kiss-warm hugs, sweet caresses and tight holdings

the Cottage wept deep sobs

as it remembered

there had been such pain with the fire, as beams broke wide and rafters crashed
furniture withered, flame veined curtains, lino globbed in tiny pustules

photos blacked out of memory, precious carvings
dissolved, keepsakes melted
and the next days dawn crept low over skeleton walls,
charred ruins and the sharp taste of ash

the Cottage healed slowly

as it remembered

after the clearance the first smudge of green in the grave-
brown earth, grassroots regrown
birds quested worms in the trenches upturned and
micelings sniffed and snuffled for seeds
lichen smoothed green the stumps of foundations, moss
ironed out cracks in walls heat-blown
and the next Spring brought colour and cubs, fur babies
and new birthed, all in Natures rebound

and life thrived and
continued, continued and thrived

as life always must

Orla McFaul

Heart Balm

In the early morning light
I sit with my heart
battered   bruised

but hopeful still
hopeful as dawn

a tentative sun peeps over the horizon
wonders what the day will bring
what the world will show

a warming sun
holds firm
weathering storm after storm

not always seen   but always there
unhurried   until dusk
then trusting the moon to take watch

two halves   one heart
in the sky
parental   custodians of our world

strong steadfast sun and misty magical moon
ruling time   tide   life
beating   clockwork

heart balm
healing for the soul
when all around is fleeting

Geraldine Fleming

Beneath Opal Skies

'That's the best bad idea I've heard so far.' Leo clapped his heavy-duty gloves signalling the end of the meeting.

'After all, we can't disappoint our families, can we? Never have before... it's not starting now.'

Glenn and Willis nodded conceding the discussion. With solemn shrugs, they strode toward the shaft's exit ladder. Tunnel spoil crackled under boot and the dry dust of recently jackhammered sandstone clung to the dense air. Their retreat was based on years of 'Leo experience'. He would want them to leave the mine, give him time to think, time to formulate. Since his collapse the future had taken a pale grey pallor, much like Leo himself.

Their hard hats broke ground level. Body sore and shading their eyes from the bald sun they set off over a pockmarked wasteland. Two giants miniaturised in the vast belly of the landscape. Sidestepping mullock heaps en route to their trailer. Usually, they would have staged a stronger resistance. Many times, anger blazed between the three brothers, hot and personal. Leo led by example, that was his motto. In the Tavern at each end of season celebration you could hear the boom of his voice as he took some newbie asking advice to task.

'Never, ever ask a man or a woman to do something

you wouldn't do yourself, Full stop.'

Now though everything was changing. Dynamics in flux, a yawning chasm as the threesome silently negotiated new lines, new dissections and new tolerances.

Alone, Leo turned to face the load-bearing wall, the focus of their discussion. Halogen lights cast his fading shadow as he paced the hewn verge. Camouflaged in apricot dust he hunkered on the floor, pushing down his new-prescribed mask he ignored ragged breaths as he ran calculations through his head. He picked a spot on the roughcast wall and stared with laser precision. Dazzling green eyes flickered and his square jaw clicked as he sketched imaginary lines and dropped in audacious figures intent on achieving the goal. A long absent smile interrupted the lines on his face, gruff hands smeared unexpected tears. He had promised himself no tears sitting in that hospital bed. The cardiac consultant stepped back between the pink cubicle curtains, leaving Leo adrift in his alternate world. He missed filler words completely but the significant parts, those life chilling phrases clung to the fog-swirl in his brain. *It's serious... heart disease...no exertion... need to change your work... talk to your family.* He marvelled so few words could change his life, his future, everything.

A brilliant engineer, Leo had no interest in the tens of millions of years taken to form opals. He did not dream like a geologist of water percolating silica through stratum of sandstone, settling in the cracks to eventually form precious gemstones. Instead, he dreamt in marvellous technicolour, opals iridescent in their splendour freed from their earthly tombs. Diffracting flashes of colour sang to his heart. Above all else though, was his heart's desire, the most beautiful, most valuable opal the enigmatic black opal.

Leo read indicators, the shorthand of stone told where to aim the jack and usually he was right. He always said hitting a good seam was fifty percent calculation, twenty-five percent intuition and the last twenty-five just sheer bloody determination.

He was an opal hunter, that was what he knew. It coursed through every cell, coded every synapse, it was his last thought at night and first in the morning.

Each season the quality of the finds sustained their families and financed the next season's hunt. They all enjoyed a good living, some years better than others. This season's finds for the trio had been scant, barely covering their overheads. Their search for the elusive opal bearing seams remained just that, elusive. Leo's absence weighed heavy on his brothers and their families. Worry lodged in everyone's heart, though with respect little was said once Leo outlined his plan. No one wanted to think about the future, remaining wide-eyed in a strange world. Admittedly the level of risk in this dig was one Leo would not have considered acceptable, not in the past. Yet he had twisted and turned in his usual emphatic manner until he got his way. In truth though, they were short on options.

In the trailer they kicked back after their first lager and a spruce -up, waiting on Leo. Glenn strummed his tuneless guitar, plucking chords like random thoughts. Willis leaned easy against the galley unit slicing and dicing vegetables. Relaxed now they reran the plan, teasing it back and forth until they felt they had their moment unclouded by Leo's conviction.

Over the years they had outvoted him only to end up squirming in regret and lighter in their bank balance.

'You remember the time you broke your leg in that landslide? Jesus, I thought Leo was going to kill us himself.'

Glenn struck a particularly discordant note as a memory pain shot through his leg.

'Well, you can understand, he did say *don't dig there*. He was specific. Lucky it wasn't worse.'

'True Wills. That leg still gives you bother.'

'You got us a shed load of bother when you used that new appraiser. Instead of Jake... all cause you thought you could get a better deal from a sheila. She ripped us off ...big time... You always were a fool for a pretty face.'

Willis tossed the rolled-up towel at his brother only to receive a slapstick return.

"Thanks... I'd finally managed to forget that, and you

bring it up.'

Glenn rested his guitar on the floor, Willis straightened the towel, an air of seriousness returned to the trailer.

'What d'you think he's doing down there?

'Just thinking, planning this stunt. Praying it works. Trying to shoulder it all himself.'

I guess, he'll come in soon to eat... Jeez I just thought about that time with the jack compressor. He was in the ballroom giving it full throttle when that bloody thing just spluttered to a dead stop. And then ... and then you tried to bluff him we'd serviced when we hadn't. God...now that was unbelievable. We let him go to Darcy's Fitters before we admitted we hadn't taken the damned thing in.'

'Yeah … and when all the yelling was done, he said it was the lie annoyed him most.'

'Mm-mm that one I never forgot.'

***

Leo was established as the voice of reason, he worked the margins well for the brothers over the years, steering close to the cliff edge, always the right side of gravity. True to his prediction his younger brothers never raised one doubt about the wisdom of removing the supporting wall.

The expense had all but cleared out their stake and savings. New pillars and props, great felled trees, wedged tight with chunks and then slimmer cuts braced the roof. Leo supervised the work and within the week they were ready. The consequence was unspoken, succeed or fail after this everything would change.

'Right then.' Willis said lifting the jack. 'Where do you want to start?'

Leo swept his torch beam over the rock surface; he knew every contour. He patted the bare rock like a friendly old dog.

'Here Willis, gentle just here... This is the sweet spot.'

They gathered in the ballroom, seventeen metres below ground. Taking out the bearing wall required the suspension of reason, old school thinking and faith in Leo. The jack hammer punched rock. Glenn began to lift and clear the spoil into the vacuum while Leo unaccustomed to this enforced inactivity stood against the wall. With each series of strikes they halted, checking the props and Leo stepped forward to rub shards off the rock face. The demolition continued in their efficient silence.

Glenn saw it first. A dark glint in the unnatural light. Howling he yanked Willis back from the wall. The jack pounded empty space in the fraction it took to release the throttle. Forgetting the warning about overexerting himself, Leo dragged the lights closer, shadows stretching the darkness left behind. He tilted one blinkered stem onto the jacked spot. There it was- unmistakable- the seam revealed itself to them. Every element in the universe spun around that exact moment, pinpointing that exact scene. This was their discovery, their God Particle, black opal.

Gently, with precision they gouged away the ancient crust of rock. All eyes locked on the wall, straining, breath held, hearts tripping with excitement... They worked and the seam expanded and expanded. Shielded from the outside, existing only in their own hollowed out world the trio pitched between awe and elation. Over two days they uncovered a record-breaking haul, enough black opal to stake many years hunting, enough to cushion financial worries.

On the third day with the seam denuded, the trio stood above ground. In the midst of a scraggy pale salmon landscape and blue opal sky the brothers gathered around the sagging appraiser's table. Jake, struggling to maintain his professional demeanour, had confirmed everything they expected and so much more. Faces streaked with tears, they whooped and hugged. Brothers united in birth and bonds. Feeling the narrowness of Leo's once sturdy frame, reminded the brothers of the seismic shift in all their lives.

Jake offered his hand in congratulations. Years of finds and haggling and respect spilled over as he was pulled into the brothers' bouncing embrace. With the haul safely locked up in Jake's ancient safe and the money transferred to their business account the only thing left was a 'deal closed' drink.

'Shall we retire to the Tavern? A drink and a bite to eat?'

Jake only had to ask once. They walked the dusty street like gunslingers, no spurs, no guns but a swagger in their step.

'Well, boys what do you think of big bro's new venture? You think he can help those newbies sort this game?

'I think *Leo Anderson Consultant Engineer* has a ring to it. They are getting a lifetime of experience from the best... the very best.'

Glenn nudged Leo's elbow.

'Show your business cards... '

Leo set a stack of pristine cream cards in the centre of the table. Each lifted one in turn., like cutting a deck for winner takes all.

'Mm-mm classy... great reference to the biggest black opal find ... to date... Holds out hope. Good selling point.'

Willis held the card moving it back and forth appraising its virtue and value.

'Look at all those letters after your name. Guess all that study wasn't wasted.'

Glenn whistled a low note of appreciation.

'Time you both tried a bit of study yourselves, use the brains God gave you. You need more than one string on a manky guitar in this life. Never know... I could be putting work your way. Remember... I'm still a partner and not a bloody silent one either.'

Leo stood proud, a different future crystallising before his eyes. He was beginning to appreciate the geologists' long perspective. When conditions align opals form, sometimes they differ in colour and grade, all are beautiful, all are unique. He raised his glass to the gathering.

' Well, isn't life strange... Seems to me there is not just one path for any of us. I sure got butt-kicked into a different world... But you know what? Sometimes forced change is what you need...what we all need. So it's cheers to change.'

Glasses raised, the gathering drank to their new world, full of potential.

'What I want to know is how will you share an office with Jake? He isn't going to pander the way we do. You won't come home to a cooked dinner every evening.'

Willis eyes danced as he enticed Leo to rise to the bait.

'Never you mind with that. We will be fine. Makes sense this way, share costs, share customers. I'll do family rates, by the way, when you need me.'

Leo winked at his brothers and further afield, a general wink at the universe of infinite change.

Ian Turnbull

Arrhythmia

betrayal plotting
unfaithfulness and lies
difficult to deal with   a deceitful heart

lost rejected
affections spurned
difficult to deal with   a broken heart

cruel harsh
passionless and cold
difficult to deal with   an iron heart

oracles aortas
ventricles and valves
difficult to deal with   a damaged heart

hope   our universal panacea

Sue Steging

Secret Hearts

Who knows the secrets
of our human hearts? Not iron
yet they forge magnetic fields,
fuel ozone layers for souls
we house in flesh
then mantle with heredity,
whispering in hidden halls
of choices made to ward off pain,
narrowing the passageways of blood.

Secrets surge like lava.
They rise to crack the crust
creating scars and wounds
washed clean with ocean's
salty tears then dressed
with fine black ash made soil.
Catastrophe recorded in a layering
of metamorphic/ metaphoric plaque.

Not clocks, hearts tick circadian,
keep time with planetary turns,
mark earth's slow passage of return
not to oblivion but to merge again,
become the stardust that brought
elements of metal and of stone to pulse
for moving flesh and bone.

Earth's secret energetic heart
moon-big, sun-hot, will cool at last.
The swirling dynamo will tire,
and geo/homeostasis will relax
while diamond-making pressure,
now relieved, will open up the earth-shell
to the blast of cosmic winds.

Until then human hearts (unmoored),
can learn to beat elsewhere,
be hearthstone to another home.
The shockwaves that unsettle
can bring us back to life
while our core sends out its energy,
like the plume of a volcano,
calling out to greet the stars.

Emma E Kane

Out of Time

My whole life I have willed time to pass. Wishing I was older, wiser, longing for the hard times to be over. Failing to appreciate the rosebush in bloom until it has returned to stick and thorn. Neglecting to notice the apples until they have long since fallen from the tree. I berate myself for being too busy to spend time with you. I did not miss you until you were a shadow.

Your lived-in face is marred by the laughter, the trauma. Every wrinkle, each broken vein, wisp of white hair is a testimony to a time in your life. I yearn for more time with you. But you are life-weary. Ready. Your days are numbered. Like sand, time slips through our fingers.

Of course, there are the memories. The times you spat on a screwed-up hanky to clean my not so dirty face. The time you got drunk on sherry, did the Can-can around the kitchen. The times I lost you in the supermarket. Deep conversations with strangers. Confidante to all and sundry. Your toothless smile. Dentures in the palm of your bony hand. Your singing. Always out of tune. Out of time.

Paul Girvan

Affairs of the Heart

Sean sauntered into the room.

"Hi Guy, how's it going - you look a bit downhearted."

Guy sighed. "It's that pretty nurse Beatrice - you know the one I fancy. She just doesn't seem interested."

"Faint heart never won fair lady. Don't lose heart, Guy. You are in with a chance.

All the nurses think you are heart throb you know. God knows why." Sean laughed.

"I have had my heart broken once too often. You know I fell for Gemma heart and soul and look where that got me. She was a real heart breaker. Nothing breaks like a heart. Just try sleeping with a broken heart! It is no fun being the owner of a lonely heart."

"My heart bleeds for your achy breaky heart Guy! I always knew Gemma was a mistake. Anyone who had a heart would have known what you were going through. But you know you have much better luck with women than me. I know women can break hearts sometime Guy but maybe Beatrice could have a change of heart. Maybe she is coming out of a bad relationship. The heart has its secrets you know."

Guy didn't look convinced. "Anyway, the news about Ukraine is really upsetting. I have a new Ukrainian sister-in-law - did you know? She poured her heart out to me on Friday and we had a real heart to heart – a terrible tale. The family back home seems to be living in the heart of darkness."

Sean nodded. "Hopefully that cold hearted tyrant Putin has met his match in Zelensky. That man seems to have the heart of a lion - he's a real latter-day Braveheart. But you're right. It is really heart breaking to watch what is going on but the heart of the matter is Putin is a cruel dictator who won't stop. The Ukrainians certainly aren't fainthearted at the moment. Let's hope they keep up their fight."

Guy nodded.

Sean went on "My heart goes out to them but in my heart of hearts I fear for the future. I nearly had a heart attack when I heard of the possibility of a nuclear attack."

Sean poured himself a cup of over boiled coffee on the trolley and took a swig. The bitter sour taste of the coffee made him wince.

Time to change the subject he thought. "Didn't I see you at the match last night? Didn't the late try warm the cockles of your heart? Our team certainly put their heart into the whole match, and it paid off. My heart stopped a beat when the number 10 was tackled but what a pass! I even shouted '*Eat your heart out*' to those baying thugs on the opposite benches when the number 6 grounded the try."

"Sean, for Pete's sake let's have a break from all these heart clichés!" said Guy.

Sean grinned. "We are cardiologists you know - what do you expect! Anyway, I suppose we should get back to work. By the way Beatrice is on your theatre team today. Maybe after the op you could take her out for a coffee or a meal but certainly don't come to this crummy place. No hearty meals here! Take her somewhere special and have a true heart to heart. Bare your heart to her - you might just steal her heart. They say she's got a big heart. Not literally, I hope. We know a thing or two about enlarged hearts don't we!" He laughed.

Guy thought for a moment. "Maybe I will give it another go, but personally I find dealing with real flesh and blood hearts a lot easier than dealing with affairs of the heart."

As Guy entered the operating theatre Beatrice in her fetching blue scrubs turned to Guy and gave him a heart melting smile. Guy missed a heartbeat and then zing went the strings of his heart. She could surely hear his heartbeat. All was not lost. He was in with a chance. The heart wants what it wants.

Mae Gardiner

Not just yet

I awake in

Hypnagogia

sensing another

heart beating

I neither asleep

nor awake held

to the ether by only

a fine Gold Thread.........

I see

the End, edging

ever nearer

..... and then the angel speaks to me.......

telling me to walk away

across the dreaming dawn

climb back down

into me

and wake

for today is

not my day

to return home

to merge with the divine

… and then my heart screams at you …

NO !

a silver spider web

glistens brightly

across a beam of light

stitching my life to yours

to what you do

what you think

what you say

our hearts mirror

shining

sparkling

splendid

and the thoughts

of love you

wrap around

us snuggly

are just a cloak

you must release

in time

to revert

to a solitary

single

heart-core

but not this time

not just yet…

Helen Hand

Peru 1980

They came home, the seven of them

Leaving my man behind on the mountain.

On a glacier, in a foreign land.

He fell, so they said.

In dreams, I didn't believe them,

In dreadful dreams, he chose not to come home,

Tired of me, tired of our children.

So he stayed in Peru, lived free, loved free.

Left us willingly.

In daylight, my mind knew the truth of his death,

But I took against those others

Who left him behind

As if they had helped him to stay there

And knew another truth.

Janet Peace

TAPESTRY

our frame crafted solid

love loomed large

together we wove woollen dreams

you were my warp

I your weft

when you were down

I was up

life threw the shuttle

left to right

» »

« «

right to left

⟵ back and forth ⟵

---------------- stacking ----------------

---------------- time ----------------

---------------- lines ----------------

your warp was taut

my weft obedient to the pull

tension finely balanced

threads spun from coarse-combed yarn

were beaten in place

patterns emerged

warp distorted

tensity slacked

weft floated free

weave unpicked

thread by thread by thread

cut loose we

U N R A V E L L E D

Brenda McAteer

Thirteen Seconds

One second

My baby girl roaring at me, shouting about her rights to go out half naked. Lucy, my diamond in the sky, aged fifteen. Doesn't want a lift home, she'd die of embarrassment if I turned up. I can't cope. Head and chest tight. Those onions at dinner too much. I take some Gaviscon, go and lie down.

Two seconds

Marianne's back from taking her mother to the consultant. Her face tells it all. I can see it's not good news. I let her cry in my arms. It's dementia. We need to start planning for Sadie's care. I go upstairs and try to calm down. Heart racing, I feel so fatigued. Splash water on my face, sit down, breathe slowly. Downstairs to offer my support.

Three seconds

The asshole of a new manager called me in today. I need to up my callouts to at least 25 a week! I'm the engineer requested by most clients because I take time over the job, listen to their woes and tidy up. What would he know? He's never been out on an actual job. In the car on the way home I start to shake, feel nauseas, sweat. My hands are glued to the wheel. I pull in, lean back, breathe slowly. Normality returns.

Four seconds

Sunday family lunch out. Lucy and Sadie on the same wavelength, a joy to watch them playing the silly games they did when Lucy was little. After lunch we go for a walk in the rose garden. Sadie clinging to Lucy. 'Slow down a bit', I call. Too late, they both take a tumble. Lucy in hysterics. I rush to help but get the most painful cramp and indigestion ever and lie curled up beside Sadie. In the end, just scratches and scabs, no broken bones. We all have a laugh about it on the way home.

Five seconds

Marianne gives off about the amount of Gaviscon I'm taking. She's also annoyed about how tetchy I've become. I shout, 'It's stress - pressure of work, negotiating a teenager, trying to get help for your Mum to keep her at home'.
'Me too', she wails. I storm off. Halfway up the stairs I double in two and half sit, half lie on the stairs. 'Right' she announces, 'You're going to the Doctor'.

Six Seconds

'Don't see you often Mark. What's the problem?' I mutter about work, teenagers, poorly mother-in-law. He

checks blood pressure, heart rate, a bit high but not bad. 'There's no need to do a BMI you're so slim'.
'I swim 40 lengths two or three times a week'.
'It's not your heart then, Mark, stress probably. I could give you beta blockers but come back in six weeks and we'll repeat the tests, just to be sure'.

Seven Seconds

The long-planned summer holiday in Alicante. Marianne's brother has moved in with Sadie for the week. Sun, sea, siestas. A trip in a glass bottomed boat to glimpse the sea life. So colourful, just gorgeous. Without warning I'm gripped by panic. Sweat pouring down my face and body. I clench Mariann's wrists in an attempt not to keel over. Back to the hotel, a cool shower and siesta sorts me out.

Eight Seconds

We're visiting potential care homes for Sadie. Two pleasant and caring but the third we wouldn't have left a stuffed cat in. The so-called adult care manager makes my work boss look considerate! All about money. There's the monthly fee, but any extras like hair dressing and outings will be charged separately. I shout, 'Can she pee for free', as I storm to the car in a rage and collapse at the wheel. I gasp for breath and pour sweat. Marianne glares at me.

Nine Seconds

'Me again Doc, now having panic attacks.' He listens, checks me out, all readings a bit higher but then I'm so stressed. He refers me on to cardiology. Just in case.

Ten Seconds

I have such a row at work with my manager. He's suggesting that at fifty-seven I should look at my options. Early retirement or an office job. I fume and go into a bit of a frenzy. Storm to the car, speed off, scrape the side panel exiting the carpark. Shout at Marianne and stamp off to bed – at 7pm.

Eleven seconds

Doc phones after I ask for a sick line. So uptight after the row with the manager I take a week off. First time in forty years at the firm. Doc says he's been speaking to cardiology and if I have another panic attack I've to go straight in as that's the best time to take readings.

Twelve seconds

We've chosen a care home. We're going to tell Sadie. I'm driving but feeling so anxious for Marianne. How are we going to convince Sadie this is good news? We stop at the last set of lights before Sadie's house and I freeze. Cars behind blaring their horns but I can't move. Heart and head pounding, sweat pouring. Marianne gets the driver behind to help drag me into the back seat. She speeds to the cardiology department.

Thirteen Seconds

I vaguely agree to an exercise ECT. Hooked up to the machine the nurse instructs me to start walking. "Let's see how many minutes you can march", she smiles.

Thirteen seconds - that's all I achieve before the nurse stops the machine, throws me in a wheelchair and takes me to the cardiac ward. Later Marianne, white as my bedsheet says, "Those weren't panic attacks Mark. More like mini heart attacks. Warnings your heart was failing – you could have died".

All my future seconds

Angina. I have angina. It all makes sense now. Can't have a stent fitted but with lifelong medication I can batter on as normal.

Not only feeling fit but I've stopped bawling at my shadow - and all my loved ones.

My Union have told work I need less stress, so I'm back to my original workload. Asshole scared to upset me, result!

My GP apologises every time we meet. He says I've reminded him slim, non-smokers who exercise can still have heart issues. Genetics and all that.

Best of all, Lucy now calls me Lucky Thirteen. She works hard to avoid setting up major incidents at home. She says she just wants to keep my heart ticking.

So do I.

Jimmy Milliken

heartscape

over and over the brow of the hill
        dance silhouette
        against a raging dawning
all tango clasp and pangs of longing

plummet burst of smoke and flame
        velocipede
        and raptor
crank and clang of laughter

waltzing through the thistle stalls
        all barb and spike
        and clouds of down
and dewy moist and spittle squall

and clung on still when tumbles cease
        and hands and hearts
        and tongues avow
as symbols shown on frosted panes

        and cracks in bowls
        and creaks in doors
and light through stained glass windows

Rhona Stephens

Greeting

she is perfect
nascent beauty
in a body ivory smooth butter soft
lash and brow sweet shadows on her lovely face
hair - a dusting -
midnight dark
and ears
mirrored perfection
formed within me - within *me*
close-curled fingers
toes a marvel of artistry
and lips parting pouting
to cry
or to suckle strong against my breast
I hold her kiss-close
surely
surely that is a whisper of breath
a first whisper against my cheek
for she is perfect!

no they say
her heart…
not possible to detect in utero…

nothing they could do…nothing I have done…
they're sorry…I'm sorry…
…not my fault they say again
and again…
and yet
I feel the need to apologise to her
again and
again and
again…
  I'm sorry…

where will my love
my words
my dreams
stored up for you
where will they go?
what shall I do with them?
stored nine months three days
No!
stored a lifetime
for I thought of you
twenty years ago
on Christmas Day when
I hugged the softness
smelt the sweetness
soothed the sadness

of my new baby doll
who did not breathe
but as I held her
was alive to me
as you are now

where will they go these sorrows
these tears for you who will
never cry
nor smile
nor laugh for the joy
of being alive
Oh… what shall I do with my tears
when the acceptable season of grief is past?

I am lost in the astonishment of grief
the slipperiness of a sorrow
that can't be
captured
contained
controlled
a sorrow with a beginning
but in this pre-dawn world
no end

Jane Avery

The Craft

To fall is an enigma.

Descent, in all its ecstasy
plays twofold – pivots like the crow.
Whoever of their number caw,
dictates the landing –
satin sheets or
adamantine.

Inhale – it's just respiratory.
Acclimatize.
This mental state's… collected,
just displaced,
sometimes euphoric -
matching heartbeats,
swift,
distended.

Unchain the anaesthesia
ascend
those ramparts don't exist
you are the only cornerstone
now starts the craft
so rise.

Image by Steven Budgen

Chris Butler

In Vein

One day my heart just up and left
from its bone and cartilage cage in my chest.

First it divorced the arteries and veins,
preventing the valves' drainage from my brain.
Then the four chambers split into two
to muscle through dense flesh and connective tissues.
The medulla oblongata tried but couldn't regulate
this vital artery's premeditated escape.

Using the aorta and cavernous venae cavaes,
my vital organ climbed higher and higher,
ascending this esophagus,
damming my rapid pulse,
causing me to convulse and cough
my myocardin right out of my mouth.

When it was gone I crawled along the floor,
following the blood trails through the back door.

Lost and Found

Every time my heart breaks, a few pieces go missing:

Between the couch cushions, under the Oriental rug,
cuddling
a dust bunny in the vacuum's belly, stuck to my shoe's
soul,
hiding inside my other pocket, locked in the vegetable
crisper,
buried beneath the egg shells and coffee grounds in the
kitchen
trash can and somewhere around the lost and found.

Every time my heart breaks, I can't find them all.

Philip Dunkerley

Gentle Goodbye

for Ricardo Kosloski, against the odds

Each day I gently say goodbye
to things and people that I love;
and though one day we all must die,
I know my love of life is true.

To things and people that I love
I leave the essence of my soul;
I know my love of life is true
and makes a broken world feel whole.

I leave the essence of my soul
to show that cancer cannot kill;
to make a broken world feel whole
I tried to do more good than ill.

To show that cancer cannot kill
I'll always be a part of you.
I tried to do more good than ill,
believe me when I say it's true.

I'll always be a part of you,
and though one day we all must die,
believe me when I say it's true,
each day I gently say goodbye.

Blackbird - Life is Really Tough

i.m Richard Tuson

Blackbird singing in the evening,
spilling liquid music from above,
I'm out walking, and believing
that I will always be somebody's love.

Blackbird singing in the evening,
sometimes, life is really tough,
sometimes hurts so much I'm bleeding,
together with the smooth you get the rough.

Blackbird singing in the evening,
wonder what the future holds for me,
it sometimes helps to do a little grieving,
a little grieving sometimes sets you free.

Blackbird singing in the evening,
confident the future will be bright,
got to learn to share the blackbird's feeling,
sun goes down but morning brings the light.

Blackbird singing in the evening,
sings as if his song'll never end,
blackbird has a very special meaning,
brings to mind a very special friend.

David Congalton

The Man in 21C

Clutching my boarding pass, I slowly made my way down the crowded aisle. The flight was full. There was excitement and anticipation in the air as the passengers settled in their seats, waiting to depart Santiago, Chile that Sunday morning. Next stop, Ushuaia, Argentina and a rendezvous with a cruise ship bound for Antarctica.

I looked again at my seat number: 21B. Another three hours trapped in the dreaded middle seat of an airplane. A small price to pay for the adventure that lay ahead.

He was already in the aisle seat, 21C. Short gray hair. Gray mustache. Glasses. Stocky in build. Staring blankly straight ahead.

"Bad news," I said, as I reached Row 21. "I'm sitting next to you." I'll never forget his response as he popped up and graciously made way.

"Good," he said, with a slight Southern drawl. "Now I'll have someone to talk to."

So we talked for the next three hours, all the way to Ushuaia. His name was Bob and he was from Atlanta, retired from the phone company after 35 years of service. 58 years old. Two adult children. Divorced. An avid scuba diver, but not exactly an experienced traveler. Like me, Bob had always wanted to visit Antarctica. We both understood that this would be the trip of a lifetime.

We got separated at the Ushuaia airport, but I saw Bob again on the ship later that day as the passengers gathered for our first dinner. My friend Jan and I were in the lounge with a couple we had just met from New Jersey. Bob came wandering through by himself. I waved him over and he ended up joining us for dinner.

That began the pattern for the next eleven days as Bob became part of our group. We had lunch together. We had dinner together. We certainly had way too many drinks together. Bob was easy to get to know, funny and entertaining. I became closer to him in eleven days than I do many friends in eleven years. We just clicked.

Our time in Antarctica was everything we wanted, and more. Neither one of us spent much time in our cabins. We were the guys outside on deck, often not bothering with a coat, snapping away hundreds of photos of icebergs and whales and penguins, constantly shouting to one another, "Can you believe we're actually here?" I had found someone more excited than I was to be cruising the bottom of the world and Bob enjoyed every second, every minute, every hour, of our adventure.

It was all over far too soon. Back to civilization. Back on the plane to Santiago. A final dinner and drinks together at the airport as we waited for our separate flights home. There were seven of us who had become particularly close. Email addresses and phone numbers were exchanged. Promises to visit were made. Bob seemed in no hurry to leave. The flight to Miami was on time. We shook hands and hugged goodbye. Then he was gone.

That was in February. We stayed in touch throughout the spring and early summer, exchanging photos and memories, both of us still in Antarctica, at least mentally. He talked about visiting us in California during the fall when he came out to visit his daughter. The emails stopped later in the summer. Bob must be busy, I decided. He was making plans. We'd see each other soon.

Then his daughter-in-law, Jennifer, called me from Atlanta. She had found my name and phone number on that piece of paper we had all exchanged at the airport.

Bob had died, she said, choking back tears. Leukemia. He was only 58.

A knot twisted hard in my stomach at the news. This couldn't be. He seemed so healthy on the cruise. When did Bob get diagnosed, I asked. Jennifer explained that she had found some test results from two years prior.

He knew.

Bob knew all along. That's why he was on the ship. He was dying and he wanted to see Antarctica while there was still time. He never said a word to any of us.

Flying out for the funeral became too impractical on such

short notice. Instead, I wrestled with a long letter to Jennifer and the rest of the family, trying to help them understand what Antarctica meant to Bob. And what he meant to all of us.

I looked again at the photos and think back to my robust friend standing out on the open deck, beaming in excitement and wonder as a mother whale and her baby frolic nearby, and it was my turn to choke up.

"He mentioned you a lot," the daughter-in-law told me. Yeah, well, I was just the guy stuck in the middle seat on the plane, somebody he could talk to, as we headed for the adventure of a lifetime.

You only get one, I guess. I'm glad Bob and I got to share ours together.

Mihaela Melnic

Loss

The stars had fled from my eyes and so had I from theirs
as if we were hiding from each other's light.
We blindly staggered each in our own universe
like extinct comets in the cold sky.
We had so much to talk about but didn't know how to
unclench our mouths;

they were whether sewn into the moments past, or hit by
the lightening bolt of death
and there were screams jammed in the throat, that went
down to the bottom of the soul.

The morning sun came and murmured me secrets of life
through threads of dust yarned from my dead skin.
I have so many red and black thoughts in the seabed of
my heart
that is crushed by the passage of the ferryman of souls.

The Secrecy Of The Heart

A thousand questions haunt you
whenever you find yourself
under domes clouded with smoke and prayers or
on ancient cobbled streets that echo voices of the past
in the shadow of the sun-scorched bell towers

but every answer is well guarded by your own conscience
in the penetralium of your heart.

Heralds of Love

A newborn's mighty cry
heralds the pure love
that winds through the cracks
of these dark times.
A break-through
with the truth in the chest.
No more sacrifice of skin is needed
for the drums.
Love thus announced
is a spiral that drills the core of everything
and shatters the impossible.
It is an invisible kiss given to vibrations
of space with extreme dynamism.
There is rhythm and mathematics in this love
devoid of outlines, of color or shape.
There is renascence and candor to it.

Hillary Griffin

End of Term

"Sister Bernadette, sister Bernadette..." I turned in response to my name being called, to see Vicki, the receptionist, running down the driveway, strands of hair escaping from her loosely tied ponytail and her voice muffled by the ever-present disposable face mask.
"Mrs Jones has just called to say she's stuck in traffic, about a mile before the Junction 15 turnoff; the radio reports say it could take half an hour to clear the backlog....so could you make sure all the chairs for the children are put out on the front lawn... somewhere in the shade would be great. And remind Father Tom that he'll be needed to do the blessing at the end of the singing, around 11.30....and if you could just make sure there's no litter in the play area," she finished breathlessly.

As if I didn't know what needed doing after how many...40...or was it 45 years of organising the play group's end of term concert. Still, Vicki wasn't to know, she had only been working in the Care Home for a few weeks, and this was the first time that preschool, parents and care home residents had been able to do anything like this since lockdown. No wonder everyone was a bit on edge.
"Don't worry, I'll sort everything out. It looks like it's going to be a beautiful day again, so the carers will be able to bring the residents down to watch."

"Yes, we'll bring a few down this morning and a few others this afternoon. Lisa's on reception duty later, so I'll be able to pop along this afternoon to listen to the children singing. My sister's twins are off to school in September, I'll miss seeing them in the play area."

"Well, I'll see you later then."

Vicki turned and walked back up the drive, leaving me to carry on into the preschool play area, a large grassy field with an array of apparatus suitable for the under 5s. What a change from those early days when we only had a few swings and sit and ride toys. The single storey pre-fabricated hall had been well maintained by Andy and his team, although we would need to start fund raising again to replace the felt roof after such a wet and windy summer.

I shook myself; there was plenty to do and no time for distracting thoughts. I stacked the chairs from the hall and checked that the children's decorated sun hats and other props for the concert were all close to the door.

"Sister Bernadette, look what I've got." Alfie bounded into the room, waving a bright red bucket and spade, followed shortly by his twin brother Jack.

"That's splendid Alfie, are you going to the seaside soon?"

"No, it's for our SONG, you know..."

"Now Alfie, don't be cheeky…I'm sorry, Sister, they're so excited about the concert, they've been up since 6 and I know we're far too early…" Vicki's sister sounded as breathless as her sibling.

"Come on boys, leave your things by your pegs and you can go out to play until your friends arrive…don't worry

Mrs Hall, they'll be fine running around outside for a little while. Enjoy your bit of peace and quiet and we'll see you for the concert at 11am."
"Thank you, Sister, these are for all of you, the boys have loved coming to preschool," and with that Mrs Hall produced a large box of Thornton's Continental from her bag, adding "I'll get off home now then."
A few minutes later, the assistant teacher arrived, followed by a stream of children and parents. No time to stay and watch the children play this morning, as I left to find Andy, and then Father Tom…and lastly the chef who would be providing refreshments. The July sun was already strong and I wished that I had put on a lighter cotton outfit.

By 11.30, the first concert was drawing to a close.
"Hungry sharks, hungry sharks," sang half of the children, brandishing their pictures of large grey sharks.
"Bye-bye sharks…do do do do do, bye-bye sharks do do do do," sang the others with gusto, hiding their paintings of little fish in their buckets. "Do do do do," echoed some of the residents who were clearly enjoying being outside, a rare treat these days. How Sister Martha would have loved this, but she no longer left her room on the Nursing Wing.
"Well children, that was the best singing I've heard this year; let's give them all another round of applause" said Father Tom in his lilting Welsh voice. As the clapping died down, he added, "Thank you heavenly Father for the sunshine, and all that we have to enjoy in this beautiful place. Bless your children as they leave us now

to take the next step in their lives. Amen"
"Thank you, Father Tom, now if you'd like to follow Sister Bernadette, we have refreshments in the upper courtyard by the car park and the children can enjoy a few minutes in the play area while you chat."
There was a rush of running feet as Mrs Jones finished speaking. While the children dashed towards the play area, I led the adults up the slope to the courtyard, feeling a bit breathless and light headed. By the time all the parents had left, there was no time to go up to the Home for lunch, so I took a couple of chef's home- made biscuits from the tray and walked back down to the play area to check that everything was ready for the afternoon session.

"Ah, Sister Bernadette, I'm glad you're back. I'm a bit worried about the children being in the sun for too long this afternoon, do you think you could find some spare sun hats? ....and some more bottles of water for the staff and Father Tom."
"No problem, Mrs Jones, I think we may have some spares in reception, I can't guarantee what size they'll be."
I turned round and trekked back up the drive; it certainly was very hot, perhaps the hottest day of the summer so far. With a quick rummage in the cupboards in the reception area, I found an ill-assorted collection of sun hats; then I set off down the corridors to the rear of the ground floor to pick up a pack of bottled water. By the time I returned to the driveway, the next group of children were already arriving and the whole session

would be repeated again.

Two hours later, the afternoon concert was successfully completed, parents and friends had clapped and smiled, residents returned to the Home after an enjoyable afternoon.
"Thank you so much…"
"It's been a pleasure to see the children growing up..."
"Georgina is really looking forward to starting school"
"Yes, we're going down to Cornwall for a fortnight, I know it will be crowded but we really need the break after the year we've all had."
Finally, the last of the parents, grandparents and carers had left, with the now tired children trailing behind, turning to look back and wave.
"Well, that all went really smoothly, thank you Sister Bernadette; if you'd like to take first pick from the flowers and chocolates, I think you deserve it" beamed Mrs Jones.
I selected a bunch of colourful home-grown sweet peas and a small pouch of Cadbury's Roses "Thank you, Mrs Jones, the children certainly enjoyed the new songs this year and I think we've given them a day to remember."
I turned and left the hall; the afternoon sun was still strong and instead of heading up the driveway, I took the path which ran between the terraced lawns in front of the old red brick Abbey buildings. Part way along was a bench, donated in memory of Sister Agnes, with a view out over the lawns dotted with shrubs and trees and on to the rolling Staffordshire hills beyond. An ideal spot to spend a few minutes enjoying the peace and quiet, whilst I got my breath back.

Vicki came running along the path. "Sister Bernadette, I'm so sorry I missed the concert, we had to call the ambulance out to Sister Martha in Room 40....she had a bad fall in the bathroom, today of all days.... And after all that, she's fine..."
Vicki stopped, Sister Bernadette's head had drooped and she hadn't stirred despite Vicki's chattering. She took out her mobile phone and called reception. "Lisa, ask the paramedics to come down here, it's Sister Bernadette..."

"I'm sorry duckie, there's nothing we can do, she's passed away. Not a bad spot to choose; her heart's just given out in this heat. You sit down and I'll get someone to bring you a cup of tea...."

Vicki nodded sadly, tears blurring her eyes as she looked out across the valley.

Eric Robert Nolan

Her Smile Was Silver Jupiter

It was a mad and spinning world in which you met her, but she was a mad and spinning girl -- so brightly and resolutely burning that she herself was celestial. There was starshine bottled up in her heart, solar winds charged the particles of her thoughts, ions in the atmosphere ignited her impulses. Her willful joy was her own burning sun.

When she was sly, her eyes were hasty comets. Her passion amassed from Saturnal storms. Her smile was silver Jupiter-- you wanted to repose over its white sands, beside the stained and rose-metal lakes of smoldering, darkening copper.

Between the spaces of her words, chasms of cosmos would occasionally open. You could stare into those depths for indifferent and measureless distances of light years -- the sublime nightmare-nothingness that Providence had made, the Forever-of-Empty-Dark. But before you could be afraid, her own gravity drew you in.

And you were glad. That such loveliness could exist in a single soul was reassurance. (The Forever-of-Empty-Dark wasn't entirely empty, after all.) And you were grateful -- grateful for her rejoinders, for the taste of her mouth on your own, for her girlish laugh, for the way that she regularly lighted a murky Earth with the moonbeams of her quiet kindnesses.

She was unstoppable. Ultraviolet rode the coronal shades of her irises, and flared in her contemplation. She blazed. Magnetic radiation murmured in her poetry. You loved her for her uniqueness in a universe of cold space, for the way that she burned and turned and burned and turned without ever slowing or expiring. When her light fell across you, you could almost believe that you, too, were spinning and illuminated. You loved her enough for the illusion alone.

You loved her more for her gravity that drew you in and held you, and for her arms that did the same.

Sultana Raza

REAL YOU

Have you touched your heart?
Have you found the pearl?
Have you reached inside?
Let your flower unfurl?

Have seen your eyes?
Seen the real light?
Buried deep inside,
That shines with all its might?

Have you drunk the wine,
That can help you soar?
That winks inside your eyes,
Hear the heavens roar?

Have you ever smelled,
The special scent you spread?
In laughter, and in pain,
On moments as you tread?

Have you felt the ache,
Deep inside your heart?
But have always known,
That healing is an art?

Have you touched the web,
That light spins all around?
In your dreams at night,
What treasures have you found?

Have you felt the pulse,
That echoes throughout earth?
To every new moment,
Helps to give birth?

Have you chewed on life,
All that's glowing bright?
Have you filled yourself,
With fresh morsels of light?

Do you know yourself,
The one behind the mask?
To find your real self,
Is that your real task?

Jim Simpson

A Lark Rises

Cows and pigs must be "rendered insensible to pain by a single blow or gunshot or an electrical, chemical or other means that is rapid and effective, before being shackled, hoisted, thrown, cast, or cut." The Humane Slaughter Act.

The bull is undone. Abigail waits for McCafferty to come and destroy him.

Her street is no tarmacadamed passage between dwellings. There are no neat terraces here, or regular, closed doors. Oh, do not imagine what lies beyond her own half-door, for shuddering will not help.

She considers her life. The deadbolt that keeps her in and the hens out, the duck waddlers and half-breed dogs. The cockerel on the dunkle, savage peckster, amber eye, flash evil of his rump.

'*You* will talk to McCafferty when he comes,' her man had said, 'seeing you won't talk to me.' Nor would she, ever.

The cockerel struts the cobbles. Stud-squirting clots. Picking his imperious way. Lifting his jaundiced feet, like he's done since the first cockerel set out to sow his seed in hens.

She has no kids, thank God, but mark the manky cats that have litters six times a year, till their insides are all squeezed out. Breeding for Ireland, and suckled to death. Poor pussy bleeding.

'That Michael's to be put down,' he'd said. 'You'll see to it.'

The street. The yard. The steaming midden in the street. The street hemmed in. Floors four feet deep in dung. Chained beasts excreting milk for the creamery. For the metal tanker man, the aproned, sterile dairymen, the cheese patters, make sure you please the man that feeds and clothes and impregnates you.

And the sheep-dipping . Lord, don't be talking. 'Hurl them in, the maggoty whores and let them splutter.' Half blinded. Trail them out. Burn the tails off them. That smell is wool-singe, woman.

'The bull is finished. That's life.'

An engine's rattle. From the half-door, Abigail watches a stranger in their street. In the sun. In the close fitting Wellingtons he wears.

'You've a bull to be destroyed?' the stranger says, 'McCafferty is laid up.' Does his voice contain a secret?

'My man's castrating pigs,' she tells him, 'he says, *I'll* have to do.'

'That's grand,' the stranger says. She hasn't asked his name.

He takes all in, like a man who knows, eyes resting on the flat-tyre trailers, the tangled, twisted buck-rakes. Rust and rot. Aroused, the cockerel crows. In the street, the stranger weighs up, sees all, knows her through the thinness her jumper. Emboldened, she does not flinch, though she's not used to strangers.

'I'll get the weapon,' he says. 'Will you show me where the bull's at?'

Michael moos from the depths, as she leads the stranger to him. As if he knows.

'He gave us fifty calves,' she says. 'Broken shoulder. Can't mount. End of. My husband does not care.'

The stranger pats Michael's head. His gentle, curly brow. 'Fifty, eh, fella?' he says. He says it well.

The stranger will load the weapon. She holds it, stock and barrel, while he removes his jacket. He wears a shirt and collar. She waits. She's seen it before. The ugliness. But the stranger speaks to Michael, her Michael, in a language she has not heard. In a tongue of softness, and the bull stops lowing, looking at her then, not in distress, she is convinced, but in a kind of straw surrender.

In the humid byre she stands close to the stranger, who takes the weapon, feeling his nearness. Sensing his pheromone. Michael is huge and trusting. A million motes dance as light shafts suddenly on his hair, turning it to butter cream, like when he was a baby, and she fed him with a bottle.

She stays with the stranger when Michael tilts and topples.

The stranger stays with her. She feels his reverence. The shared after-moment that could become a lifetime. They do not speak.

Later, in the corrugated, raggy, cat-meow street, the stranger makes to leave. But slowly. She walks him to his jeep. Sees him pack the weapon. Listens for the final piston throb, until, on the brae, rising, and through the wildness of whin blossom, his vehicle rounds the bend.

In this rare moment, she fills her lungs, shuts out the squeal of pigs, for on distant hills, red heifers graze, and somewhere close by, a lark ascends.

William Ogden Haynes

Saturday Morning

I've always enjoyed a slow Saturday morning, reading the
newspaper, and drinking coffee before deciding what I was
going to do on the weekend. On Saturdays, my wife would

usually go bargain hunting, and leave me to my writing, some
project, or mowing the lawn. I used to wait for her to come
downstairs, and always knew when it was about to happen.

She would always put on her jewelry last, and I would hear
her ebony jewelry box on the bedroom dresser plinking *Fur
Elise*. Then she would appear, nicely dressed, and accessorized,

going to somewhere or other, giving me a fresh toothpaste kiss
on her way out the door. And in the afternoon she would come
home looking guilty, with shopping bags bulging like ripe fruit,

and explain to me all the good deals she had found. And she
always spoke of other items she didn't buy, vowing to go back
the next Saturday to snap them up if they were still there. But

this time, she never did. She used to take Saturdays for granted
and thought of life as an endless train of days, that would just
keep coming, without ever passing her by. But she was wrong.

That evening as the moon rose sweet as an apple, I stood outside
the emergency room in the chilly air, smoking my first cigarette
in twenty-years. I could hear a train whistle receding into the

darkness, and by the time I went back inside, just like the train,
she was gone, leaving me and next Saturdays bargains behind.

Cookies

The old woman lived alone and at age ninety had few friends except
for her cat Tippy, named for the white patch of fur at the end of his tail.
She had little to offer the world anymore, but she loved baking cookies

for the neighborhood kids. The group of seven-year-olds knew that on
Wednesdays she would always bake cookies and they came every week
like clockwork to knock on her back door. She would appear on the little

screened porch in a faded housedress and proffer chocolate chip, peanut
butter and sugar cookies in tins lined with waxed paper. And while eating
cookies, the children would always pet the cat, as he flipped over on his

back and let them scratch his tummy. In the early years the children would
bring toys and drawings to show the old woman. She would always *ooh*
and *ahh* over a new squirt gun, an "A" on a spelling test or a finger-painted

masterpiece. As they got older, they would give her demonstrations with slingshots, Frisbees and BB guns while she sat admiringly in the porch swing. Then gradually, they stopped coming, distracted by other things like baseball,

soccer, computer games and the burgeoning social lives of teenagers. With the children grown and Tippy long gone, she eventually stopped baking. And today, she pushes a walker down the nursing home hallway on the way to

the dining room for an afternoon snack. Now, at ninety-six, she is tiny with eggshell bones and footsteps gentle as heartbeats. Her complexion is pale as mother of pearl and her white hair is pulled back into a whisk-broom ponytail.

She bites into a chocolate chip cookie and takes a sip of milk, not recalling that she baked cookies years ago. Then, although she doesn't know why, she has a recollection of children playing in a back yard only vaguely familiar.

It takes her a moment to recognize her daughter who has stopped by the dining room for her weekly visit. They will sit here having milk and cookies together every week until the inevitable end, which will come both too soon and too late.

Workshop

Most days, she wants to spend time in the back yard,
because it was the domain of her late husband. She
sits in an Adirondack chair he built, sipping a glass

of chardonnay, watching the bees pollinate the flowers
he planted. On this day, breeze-tossed fronds of
pampas grass sway to the twitter of chickadees,

and on the pink adobe fountain he built, a sun-lazy
lizard basks undisturbed. In her husband's vegetable
garden, a box turtle struggles along under his burden

among large, vine ripe tomatoes, green peppers
and squash. There are melons the size of volleyballs
and the unshucked ears of corn hide yellow kernels

swollen in their sockets. Her husband built a workshop
next to the garden, where he made bluebird houses,
wind vanes of geese twirling their wings, fountains,

yard art, bird feeders, and a house for the family dog.
She remembers him working there late into the night,
beneath the warm glow of halogen lights, a tape of

Johnny Cash or Merle Haggard playing in the
background.
Some evenings, she would bring a sandwich and a
thermos
of coffee to the workshop, full of the smell of freshly cut

oak from the table saw, and the sweet, acrid scent of
varnish.
He would always take the time to chat with her and show
her
what he was building. And before she left, she would
brush

the sawdust from his shirt and trace a sensual calligraphy
on his sweaty bare forearm with her finger, while telling
him with a flirty look, to come in soon and take a shower.

But today, while she enjoys the flowers, the garden,
and all the things he built, her mind always returns to
the abandoned shop that now sits empty as a broken
heart.

Patricia M Osborne

A Different Kind of Love

Our teenage love
was sealed by vows

but baby years and adolescents
ruffled feathers in the family nest.

The ties we shared remained –
just a different kind of love.

When your heart stopped
it left a rip in mine

and as you left this world
you sent a robin to remind me
of the memories we'd once made.

Dance with me

We met at the clock tower
Saturday nights.

Soft lights shone,
we glided, zigzagged,
slow slow, quick quick, slow
to Syd Dean's big band.

We jived, hopped,
I twirled over your shoulders,
through your legs.

You popped the question,
we sealed our pledge
with a tinge of lychee
in Martini with cake.

But now no more dance of love
or promenades

just the slow,
  slow beat
    of your

fading   heart.

Jan Spooner

Ghost Wind

Scattering twigs and dead leaves,
like someone who cannot sleep
you moan in the eaves; you shed

tears on the lawn or is it raindrops
glistening on crushed grass?
Who is it listening, deep in the hedge,

rustling, as the edge of the world
drains blood crimson from sight?
Why does the doorbell chime

a slow echoing tune like a long-lost rhyme
but nobody stands on the shadowy step?
Your night sighing sifts and snatches

the curtain from my mind, revealing once again
the agony of loss. You whisper with that voice
and breathe that old familiar scent. Conspirator.

Kac Young

Good Days; Bad Days

A Lost Love.

If I look straight ahead out my window I can see the Pacific Ocean, and the Channel Islands. The view spreads out like a lazy dog basking in the sunshine. If I look out the windows to my left, my eyes travel across an ample spread of plastic bags and boxes filled with my beloved's belongings. I can't even begin to count the bags and boxes stacked up on the patio waiting like brave soldiers for the charity van to collect them. It's impossible to look at them for long though because tears fall from my eyes and my heart aches all over again.

We were married for twenty years. It doesn't seem possible that she's not here, sitting at the breakfast table, telling me about her day ahead and asking me about mine. It was so sudden. There is blame, or I should say accountability, needed but none of that will bring her back. Torn between happy memories from the past, and her belongings on the patio, I still am unable to make any sense of it.

She was a minister at a progressive, New Thought church in Burbank, CA., a mother of three, divorced from her third husband. I walked into her church in 2001 straight from my own divorce attorney, with the exit papers still warm from the copy machine in my purse.

I had been a supporter of Religious Science for 20 years including the televised version on air. Since her church was only a mile from my house, it was a safe risk for me to sit in the back row, where I could sneak out and pick up my dry cleaning across the street if the sermon was tedious.

When the service began, Reverend Marlene, a petit redhead just like me, came bounding up the center aisle with practitioners following behind her, singing, and clapping to the music, "Celebrate." She took her seat on a chair on the stage, smiling broadly at the congregation while a singer opened the service with a familiar tune, "I Believe in Love." Her smile lit up the entire church and exuded a warm welcome to all.

Affirmative prayers were presented, followed by an uplifting reading, and then Marlene stepped up to the plexiglass podium and gave her talk. Not only was she gorgeous, but she had a healthy sense of humor and conveyed her message with style and class. I was surprised by how much I enjoyed the hour and felt uplifted myself.

As the congregation filed out of the church, Marlene was at the back door smiling her winning smile, shaking hands, and giving out hugs. The entry was buzzing with people picking up literature, exchanging hellos and heading down to the recreation room in the basement for coffee and donuts.

I told her I would definitely be back and complimented her on her talk.

During the succeeding months, I signed up for a refresher course in The Science of Mind, (not to be confused with Scientology.) When the series was over, I offered to host the closing social event at my home for the group. Some objected. They were used to having a potluck in the church basement. Marlene stepped in and asked them, "Why don't we accept this gracious offer?" They rescinded their objections quickly and carpooled to my house, up the hill. My house featured a lot of glass, a view of the valley with a pool and jacuzzi in the back yard. It looked particularly beautiful when illuminated by 100 votive candles.

My best friend was a caterer, she supplied noshes and

mouth-watering desserts. The guests appeared to enjoy themselves. When the last guest had departed and the caterer had packed up and gone, Marlene came over to thank me and she asked one simple question, "Who are you?" I laughed and asked her how long she had, and we ended up talking until 2 AM. I knew it was 2 AM because the timer on the sprinkler system had gone berserk in a power outage a month ago, and now watered at two instead of six AM.

We discovered that we had many things in common. We were both good talkers and patient listeners. Which was good because we both had stories worth telling and listening to.

Our relationship took six months to bloom. We discussed our growing up years, our mothers, I learned her father had died when she was five, and our school years. I learned we had the same teacher, Sr. Ruth Marie Gibbons. Marlene went to the Immaculate Heart High School where Sr. Ruth taught drama. I went to the college 10 years later, when she ran the theatre department at Immaculate Heart College. Sr. Ruth encouraged Marlene to go into speaking and debate. She encouraged me to tone it down a notch.

I stayed in touch with Sr. Ruth for 40 plus years, and

although Marlene had lost touch with her, she carried around a letter Sr. Ruth had sent her in 1961.

Having Sr. Ruth as mentor was a fairly rare phenomenon. Not long after Marlene and I met, Sr. Ruth was having a 50-Year Golden Anniversary in the same high school as Marlene had attended. Sr. Ruth had coached Marlene on the opening address for the Nuremberg trials, for which she won the speech contest that year. I invited Marlene to attend. It became our "first date."

There were other events during the summer. I purchased a box at the Hollywood Bowl for classical music nights. I invited Marlene to attend several times that summer. The music was superb, and we enjoyed ourselves. After the concert we would come back to my house, have another glass of wine, and talk until the sprinkler went off at 2 AM.

After five months of socializing and me showing up in church sitting now in a front row seat, it became obvious that ours might be more than a casual friendship. She was such a delight, a brilliant speaker and authentically loved her work.

A few people in the church suspected our relationship and clustered in small groups mastering the stink-eye grimace. We never announced anything formally, let them figure it out. Besides, it was genuinely none of their business.

One early fall night, when we were enjoying our in-depth conversation, Marlene braved the question, "What shall we do about our relationship?" I was surprised at the candor of her question, but not my feelings for her. Without much of a pause, "We go to Paris," I replied. "Oh, I can't go to Paris," she protested. "You have vacation time every year, don't you?" I asked. "Well, yes, but I can't afford to go to Paris," she defended. I leaned in and said softly, "I have two first-class tickets to any destination in Europe, how about I pay for the trip, and you just get the time off." She was overwhelmed, excited, and said, "Deal." (It was true. I had two first class tickets left over from the tenth anniversary trip I refused to take my cheating ex-husband on.)

We went to Paris in the spring, and since I had spent a year there after college, I was able to show her the sites almost like a native. We had a ball. We stayed at a wonderful hotel, she mastered the Metro, and we got haircuts, dyed our hair bright red and walked around like we owned the city. It was a fabulous trip. We couldn't wait to go again, and so we did. The following fall when she got another vacation.

Health Challenge

The next spring, she became very ill. During the winter she developed symptoms of a cold that wouldn't go away. It progressed quickly into pre-pneumonia because she pushed herself hard to keep up with all the required demands of a church minister. Her doctor kept prescribing antibiotics and after the ninth round of the same old pills, I stepped in and insisted she find a new doctor.

I was working on my PhD for natural medicine at the time, and I knew something was terribly wrong.

On June first of that year, she went to bed feeling terrible. She didn't arise until July 3rd. During that time, she would have terrible shivers followed by a raging fever, the same symptoms a person with malaria has. I changed the sheets 6-7 times a day, for a month. Marlene was incapacitated for making calls, so I got on the phone with assorted doctors and nurses until I finally convinced one of them to listen and make her an appointment for an examination. After the exam and x-rays, the new doctor thought polyps on the ethmoid frontal sinuses might be the culprit. He scheduled an OR right away to remove them.

The surgery was successful, or so he said, but it resulted in the complete loss of her taste and smell receptors which lasted the remainder of her life. He gave her a referral to a respected rheumatologist, an infectious disease doctor and a hematologist. It took 18 months, a five-day hospital stay, a lung biopsy surgery, and seven specialists to diagnose the true cause which turned out to be extremely grave and hideous, Wegener's Granulomatosis.

Wegener's is an autoimmune disease that inhibits blood flow to some of the body's organs. It causes inflammation called granulomas, which can surround the organs working from the sinuses down the body to the liver and consecutively cause them to malfunction. Untreated, Wegener's is fatal. The treatment to maintain and curtail the disease from spreading comes from the family of chemotherapeutic drugs.

Her energy was sapped, her spirits dampened, but somehow, against all odds, she summoned her strength, rose to the occasion, decided to reclaim her church that had been supported by guest speakers while she healed.

The nature of Wegener's is that it comes and goes in waves. After a five-hour chemotherapy infusion treatment, the patient is reasonably well for a few months and then begins to sink again until the infusion can be repeated. For the entire length of our marriage, Marlene battled this unbelievably stupid condition, and my job was to help her manage it, including chauffeuring her to doctor's offices, to labs for tests, and researching new and better doctors as we proceeded on the path towards healing.

Betrayal

The church congregation and leadership became increasingly impatient with her need to reduce her speaking schedule. One time in 2005, while she was in the hospital undergoing another set of exploratory tests, they asked for her resignation. Instead of banding together to help fill in the gaps of her absence and leadership, they wanted her gone. This beloved, cherished, vivacious, and dedicated minster who grew the church from 40 to 1200, was effectively kicked to the curb by a board who thought they knew what was best for the church. They even lied to her and hired someone behind her back to take her place before the ink was dry on her coerced resignation.

The wound inflicted by this betrayal continued to cause her pain, a hurt far deeper than Wegener's could ever match. She did her best to forgive them. She processed the hurt over and over and rationalized that "they" were doing the best they could. She tried not to blame them, only forgive them. Yet, it was the biggest blow to her calling and her essence that would ever befall her. For the rest of her life nothing would ever replace this wrong or heal the damage it did.

I suggested that we move out of town, away from the danger of running into the offenders at the grocery store and far away from the pain. All she had ever wanted to do was serve and love her congregation.

When she became ill during our second trip to France, I remember sitting by a pond with her and tears streaming down her face, she confided, "All I ever wanted to do was love them."

We moved four hours up the coast into a house in Cambria, by the sea, deep within the woods, surrounded by gorgeous oak trees and Cambria Pines. Marlene loved the forest and I believed she might heal there in that forest.

Before our moving day, on one of our nights at The Hollywood Bowl, I found myself out of breath walking up the hill that was usually easy as pie. This particular night, I couldn't catch my breath. I phoned my doctor the next day to let her know. After I explained my symptoms, her nurse instructed me to go directly to the ER

I didn't take this as seriously as I should have and said I would go the next week. The doctor called me back and said, "Go now." Marlene took the summons more gravely than I did and managed to convince me to get in the car. As usual, she was right. The next morning, I was scheduled for a treadmill stress test, which I didn't pass so they booked me into the Cath Lab and two stents were implanted. (The Cath Lab is a designated OR where stents are implanted, and minor heart repairs are done.)

I had seemingly dodged a bullet. But, in the recovery room, Marlene was by my side and refused to leave me. At one point, I began to lose consciousness and speak in gibberish. She immediately hunted down a nurse who replied, "I'll be there in a minute." Marlene said, "No, you come now." It turned out that I was bleeding, profusely from a puncture that the tech had not sealed from the IV tube. Not a little bit either, I was lying in a pool of quarts of blood. Much chaos ensued and Marlene was told to leave the room while they revived me. I can remember hearing her say, "Not on your life." Good call. She had just saved mine.

In Cambria it was quiet, peaceful, beautiful, and calm. We could sit outside under an old oak tree and listen to nature. It was bliss. The house had a deck that wrapped around the perimeter giving us several vantage points and views. We made friends with squirrels, families of deer that grazed on our two acres and a rafter of turkey who proudly marched up and down the driveway with their tail feathers fanned out favoring us with a daily parade.

Health Challenge

One day in 2014, I felt an onset of the same symptoms I had felt nine years prior, shortness of breath, trouble breathing while walking, and prickly pains in my chest. The cardiologist's response was to go back into the Cath Lab for a look-see. What he found was a strange clog that the camera could not bypass, so he decided, on the spot, to perform a triple bypass.

Marlene recalled sitting in the waiting room expecting my one- hour scheduled procedure to be over by nine AM, when the surgeon came out and told her they were going to do a triple bypass, and to please make herself comfortable for the next seven hours. Marlene was scared. What if I didn't make it? How would she cope? She got on the phone quickly, extended our pets' care in Cambria and found a motel for the week. It was as traumatic for her as it was for me. I didn't come to full consciousness for another 5 hours after surgery.

Marlene stayed by my side every day henceforth and helped me recover from the physical trauma of a sawed-open chest and a large vein extracted from my right leg. This surgery wasn't easy to recover from. Fortunately, the lovely Marlene had plenty of both during the six weeks it took for me to feel anywhere close to human.

During my recovery, I decided I needed to seriously change my life and I began a regimen of dietary changes and exercise. My cardiologist had told me that condition was genetically inherited and there wasn't much I could do about it. "Let's change that," I told Marlene. She agreed to help.

I decided to write a cookbook that detailed my new approach to heart healthy foods. Instead of relying on kelp flakes and seaweed, I found new ways to switch out harmful ingredients with heart-healthy ones and retooled old-favorites in an innovative and heart-supportive way. I cooked every dish grandma ever made, designed new recipes from family favorites while diminishing or replacing the saturated fats, salt, and sugar. Marlene tasted every single dish with me after I had meticulously photographed the final product. We ate well and had a ball. She often said that the revised dishes felt lighter and tasted better than the original ones. Success!

The cookbook was our pride and joy. Marlene took a special online design class to learn how to layout and design the pages for printing. She did a gorgeous and professional job, and I was grateful to have a talented partner to support me in spreading the word about heart health.

For the next few years, I travelled around the west coast giving lectures and making samples of the heart-healthy cuisine. It turned out that this little project would have dramatic effects on our lives.

We were quite happy in Cambria for 10 years but driving back and forth to Los Angeles to see our respective doctors and Marlene's health maintenance got to be a burden after a while. We decided to move to Ventura, a small town, closer to LA. Wegener's Granulomatosis required special attention and monitoring from doctors specializing in rare conditions.

Financial Loss

The real estate market crashed just as we decided to sell. Not only that, but I learned that my faithful financial advisor was being brought up on charges because she had fraudulently drained, not only my investment accounts, but those of eleven other clients. It appeared that my entire thirty years of hard work and careful investments were gone. She had mis-invested millions, coinciding with the devastating market crash of 2008 and 2009.

Suddenly, overnight, we were broke. Millions of dollars disappeared through her haphazard management and her deceitful lies. We had no alternative but to sue the brokerage firm as our monthly income was gone and we had nothing to rely on but ingenuity and Marlene's wedding revenues.

Marlene had wisely created a wedding officiant business and did fairly well since Cambria was known as a destination for weddings and receptions. She was popular.

All of our plans were suddenly put on hold. I scrambled to figure out what we would do, what we could sell and how we would live.

Both of us were shocked at the crimes this advisor woman perpetrated. She had called us friends and sisters and then purposefully betrayed us. It was unfathomable. We couldn't sleep. We paced and hoped inspiration would come floating in from the heavens.

While we waited for the paltry settlement, we scrimped and saved and lived on clever recipes featuring rice for five years.

We were finally able to sell the house in Cambria, at another loss, and buy a home in Ventura with the remaining funds. It was smaller, but we were happy by the sea and closer to our doctors. Just when we got the final repairs done and were feeling darn good about the changes, we were caught in the Thomas Fire in December of 2017.

The Natural Disaster

We had been watching television at 7:30 PM that night when the power suddenly went out. We had been advised on the news that there was a fire in the city of Santa Paula, 35 miles south of us. The wind was blowing very hard that night, at a rate of 50 MPH, but we went to bed at 10:30 PM confident we weren't in the path.

That was a mistake. At 11:15 PM a neighbor pounded on our door and told us to evacuate. I was in shock and dashed out onto our patio to see what was going on. In that instant, I saw eighty-foot-high flames lapping against the back yard fence.

The park next to us was ablaze and the fire was headed our way. I woke Marlene and told her we had to go. We hustled our five cats and two dogs into their carriers and piled into the car with them. We didn't have time to grab anything but our cell phones, purses and scrambled out in our nightgowns, slippers, and robes. I drove due west to the water's edge. We got out of the car, looked back to the hill where our home was and saw thirty miles of hill tops blazing with angry flames. The ring of fire stretched from Santa Paula to Santa Barbara, a full 50 miles. It was the most beautiful and most horrifying sight that I will never forget.

Because the power was out in the city as protection for us citizens, we couldn't check into a hotel until the power was restored because the check-in systems and computers depend on electricity to work. At five AM we finally got into a room with hungry pets who were also dazed and confused. The next morning a big-box store became our savior for cat and dog food, clothing, toiletries, and snacks to curb our hunger.

We waited four tense days to find out if we still had a house or not. Twenty-two houses on our street had burnt to the ground. For some miraculous reason, we were spared. We lost the backyard and part of the garage and kitchen walls, but nothing like the carnage that surrounded us. We were lucky, grateful, and completely in shock.

The Miracle

One year after that trauma, on a routine trip to my cardiologist, he said we needed another trip to the Cath Lab.

This time he was the one to be surprised. During the procedure, he kept me semi-awake in twilight sleep. He ran three different cameras up through my arteries because he could not believe what he saw. He discovered, with the cameras, that my heart valve, the one they had bypassed five years before, had totally healed, had reattached itself to my heart, and was pumping blood like a champ. The other veins that had "bypassed" this damaged valve were hanging limp and inactive.

His exact words, "I've never seen anything like this. I've heard about it in med school, but I've never seen it happen in a real person." He was so excited that he called in other surgeons and cardiologists and they filled the small OR to view the miracle healing. My heart had apparently healed itself and I give full credit to heart-healthy eating and exercise.

My cardiologist ran out to the waiting room and gave Marlene the good news. He was still in shock yet bursting with delight. Marlene was ecstatic. They allowed her into recovery with me. We both cried. It was a huge victory and I thought to myself, "She's next. She gets to be healed, too."

We went home a few hours later and were relieved. We had been through so much grief, anger, frustration, and sadness in the previous years, we allowed this moment to wash over us like a celebration. And it was. We had survived, we had figured things out together and we were there for each other in our darkest days. Now we were good to go, and we planned a European trip to celebrate our joy when the pandemic ended.

The Final Blow

In January of 2022 Marlene caught Covid. Her rheumatologist neglected to tell her that the infusions she was taking to contain the Wegener's wiped out the efficacy of her vaccines. She was twice vaccinated and boosted but she was totally unaware that she had no protection from the virus.

Nothing the doctors did could save her. She anguished on a ventilator for five weeks until I used my power of attorney to release her from the struggle. It should never have happened. Her doctor was negligent. Her death could have been prevented.

On my darkest days I wallow in disbelief. On the better days, I find gratitude for the twenty glorious, fun years we had together.

I know I am not alone. So many have lost loved ones in this pandemic, and I grieve their losses, too. I make an intention every morning that I will indeed survive this. That there is a reason and a purpose to her death and to my life beyond this loss.

I do not purport to know all the answers, I only know what works for me. Prayer helps, talking to her spirit keeps me sane, interacting with our pets heals my heart, uplifting books help, and tears. I cry a lot. Whenever I am completely sad, I stop for a minute and listen to my heartbeat. She helped me heal that heart. She was my reason for living and I must go on to prove she was right. I am still alive and therefore I must be meant to do something good. For her sake and mine.

Mal Leicester

Meeting Mr Silver

I ate my lunch on the Hub's terrace overlooking the River Slea. Gentle river light touched the ripples on the water and several ducks sailed serenely by. To my delight a mother duck followed by her six tooth-achingly sweet balls of yellow fluff swam into view. Quickly I snatched up my camera and took several photographs of them.

At last I picked up my handbag and rose to go inside the Hub for an afternoon photography workshop but noticing that the man who had been sitting at the next table was hurrying off having left a book behind. I called to him, picked up his book and moved forward to hand it to him.

He turned. He was tall, stooped and very thin. His face was pale, almost white with the skin stretched tight over sharp cheekbones. He had deep-set dark eyes with rather long silver hair swept back from his brow.

'Thank you, my dear,' he said, in a whispery voice, smiling at me as he took his book.

He hurried off, his silvery coat swirling around him like a cloak, almost the same metallic colour as his silver hair. In my mind I christened him 'Mr Silver'.

After an interesting workshop I walked to my lodgings nearby. I had decided not to travel home until the following day. To be honest, I wasn't anxious to get home. My life there was rather drab at the moment. Nothing exciting ever seemed to happen and it was as if, following the recent death of my flatmate, that sadness has seeped into the fabric of the place; anxiety seemed to tighten round my chest every time I walked in.

That evening I pocketed my small torch and slinging my night camera over my shoulder set out for a walk by the river. Passing several houses I continued along the pathway which was inset with several mosaic artworks of notable Sleaford places. Before long I came to a place called The Nettles, an enclosed grassy area with some interesting benches. In the semi darkness it seems a magical place, set apart from humdrum ordinary life. Here secret things could happen – good and bad.

I was snapping one of the benches, made from curved metal like frozen waves, when I noticed that two men had come into the ring of grass and were watching me; two bulky dark shapes, their coats blacker than the surrounding night.

'Nice camera,' one of them said, his words slightly slurred. They began to walk towards me.

'Let's have a look then,' one of them said, reaching to pull the camera off my shoulders. I pulled back and he slipped, falling onto the muddy grass.

'No need for that, bitch," he shouted, sounding furious.

As he stood, the other man moved closer, threateningly and I felt afraid. My camera contained several months of precious work and I was worried that they would take it or hurt me or both.

I sensed someone behind me and turned surprised. I had not seen anyone there. It was Mr Silver. He glided in front of me and stared at the two men. They gaped at him, horror on their faces, and ran away as quickly as they could.

'Come,' whispered Mr Silver. 'I'll walk back with you.'

It didn't occur to me to wonder how he knew where I had come from. I was just pleased to have his company back down the pathway. We didn't talk much, but it was a comfortable silence.

When we reached the pub where I was staying Mr

Silver stepped back to let me go in. I turned round to thank him but he had already gone.

That night, when I was ready for bed, I picked up a book that was on the bedside table.

The Ghosts of Sleaford it said on the cover. One chapter was entitled: *Mr Silver the saviour.*

I turned to the relevant page and read:

Mr Silver is a Sleaford ghost who is rarely seen. He tends to appear in the vicinity of the River Slea, usually to help someone in a difficult situation. This is why he has come to be known as Mr Silver the saviour.

There were two pictures on the page, side-by-side. One was of Mr silver as I had seen him. How had I known that he really was called Mr Silver? I wasn't horrified that he was a ghost. I would never be afraid of my saviour. I was grateful to him, excited to have met him and to heve had an unusual adventure.

It just shows, you never know when there may be something exciting round the next corner!

The other picture was Mr Silver with his face inside his dark hood, shown as the face of a skull, the frightening face no doubt seen by the two men. No wonder they had fled! I would always be sorry that I had not taken his photograph. What a wonderful portrait it could have been. I imagined his two profiles, Janus like, facing in opposite directions. I wondered if he chose which face to manifest or that he knew that people would see his good face unless they were ill intentioned. As Janus is the God of change and transition I thought that perhaps seeing his good face could encourage my progress to a happier state of mind.

I slept well that night, enjoyed my cooked breakfast the next morning and drove home with a feeling of quiet satisfaction. I had enjoyed the photography workshop, had taken some good shots of light on the River Slea and, best of all, I had met Mr Silver who somehow had comforted my heart.

Maureen Cullen

The Locket

The stranger who passed for his wife was talking. 'The money's in the account.' She was focused on her phone, a satisfied smirk on her face. A face he used to find quite lovely, with her translucent skin, and viridian green eyes that used to remind him of a fox, but now conjured up the image of a lizard.

'So soon.' It was a surprise her grandmother's estate had been finalised so quickly. He took a Pilsner from the fridge, opened it, and slugged half, thankful he wasn't on call this weekend. Memories of his day in theatre intruded but he swigged them away with the lager.

'There wasn't any other beneficiary.' She slid the phone into her large patent Gucci bag and shook one foot after the other out of her high heels whilst leaning awkwardly on the kitchen stool. A few inches in height dropped off. Now she wasn't quite so intimidating.

He wiped away dregs from his mouth. 'What are you going to do with the legacy? It's a tidy sum.' He omitted to say she didn't need it, not being short of cash as a successful businesswoman, a partner in an accountancy firm in the city.

She sidled in stockinged soles to the fridge,

immaculate in knee-length black skirt and tucked-in white silk blouse. After pouring herself a Chardonnay, she sloped against the fridge, hemming him in at the sink. He'd have to face her to pass, and he felt like a slob in his joggers and Celtic top. His eyes fastened on her figure, the slim waist and full hips. He turned, moved to the window, and stared out.

They were in a flat in the west-end, part of a Georgian townhouse. It cost a fortune, everything he had and some of hers put down as a deposit. The mortgage caused his pulse rate to accelerate.

Friday evening in July and Glasgow was bustling. On the Byres Road, to the left of his tree-lined street, students gathered outside a series of pubs and restaurants, many newly fronted by café style seating. One young couple sat on a stone wall holding hands, chatting animatedly. It had been months since he and Gail had shared a close conversation. Months since they'd walked together arm in arm or, as she preferred, hand in hand, whilst he cringed as a middle-aged Scot, palm itching for release. He'd known she could be acerbic but back then that hadn't extended to him, he'd felt special, chosen, lucky.

Sipping her drink, Gail rolled her eyes. 'Who'd have thought the old hag had that kind of money.'

Ben considered himself a mild-mannered man but at this moment he could have pressed his thumbs hard into her diaphanous neck. And he, a doctor committed to the prolonging of life. His dad would have been ashamed. He'd done good, a working-class lad from the east end, armed with nothing but his own brain and his dad's values. 'Aye, son, never you mind the rest o them, you keep tae yer ain path and remember where ye came frae.'

'Gail, you're talking about your own grandmother.'

She was so intolerant of anyone who hadn't 'made it.' He supposed she'd realised that he hadn't made it, and decided he wasn't worth her attention. Well, he hadn't made it, in monetary terms at least. He'd spent too much time with Doctors Without Borders to consider his own advancement.

Ben was rewarded for his challenge by a pointed stare and a twitch of her nose as if to belittle him. 'I know the relationship, darling.' The emphasis implied he was anything but her darling. 'I was called into the solicitor's today.'

'Why?'

'He had an envelope to give me. With strict instructions it was to be handed to me directly. Just like the old bitch…'

'Gail,' he admonished.

She ignored that. 'The old bitch had secrets, always tried to make a mystery out of nothing. Mad old bat.'

Ben sighed. 'She wasn't mad, just eccentric. I liked her. She loved you, missed you.'

'Rubbish, what would you know? She thought she was a white witch or something, living in the countryside, growing God knows what poison in that wasteland of a garden.'

Actually, it had been a wilderness garden, some of the planting allowed to grow to waist height where you could move through swathes of red poppies intermixed with oxeye daisies, creamy white meadowsweet, and five-foot high purple foxglove. Grannie Isla had taught him the flowers, name by name, and their medicinal qualities. He'd been fascinated by her knowledge.

It was on his 'Can I have your granddaughter in marriage?' visit. Isla had taken his hand and insisted they walk into the garden. He'd held back but she'd pulled him in, surprisingly strong and nimble for a 75-year-old. She knew the pathways to take where there were boundaries. It had been one of the most surreal times of his life, strolling with an ageing hippy in her long skirt, floral blouse, and sandals through a maze of dappled light shifting in a kaleidoscope of colour. He could hardly remember it all, but it returned in dreams, though when he dreamed, it was Gail's 's eyes that teased him on, her sun-dappled breasts and her swaying dimpled hips always out of reach of his eager hands, her body twirling in and out of long grasses, fiery auburn hair gleaming.

When he'd returned to the cottage with Isla, he'd been sweating and breathless. Isla had laughed, tapped his chest with her sharp nails, and said, 'You'll do.'

He was no longer sure that he would do. His children hadn't been happy with his marrying again, but he'd put that down to their resentment of someone taking over from their mother. Hell, they were grown-ups, but he should have listened. A middle-aged man losing his head over a gorgeous young redhead.

Gail opened a small square jewellery box. Her prettiness collapsing as she scowled, she moved forward a few feet and passed the box to him. Inside was a beautiful heart-shaped gold locket encrusted with diamonds.

He held the box to the evening sun and the gems sparkled. 'Are these real?'

'Apparently.' Now perched on a stool, she flicked her wine glass in a toast.

'Does it open?'

'No. I've tried. Rather glad of that. Imagine how awful if there was a lock of her hair inside or a photo. How dire!' She shivered.

'Gail.' He raised his voice.

'I'll wear it tomorrow, then I'll sell it.'

'Have you no respect?' He clicked the box shut and handed it back to her.

'And as for the money, I think I'll invest in a new Mercedes.'

'Dear God, Gail, your grandmother will be turning in her grave.'

She laughed, a derisory smirk on her face. 'No chance, she's ashes now.'

Ben inched around the central worktop, bottle in hand, and retreated to his study. He heard her call after him. 'Pizza all right later?'

'Sure,' he replied with a sigh, knowing he'd be the one putting the meal together.

He fell into his leather wing chair and glanced at the mess. He was allowed this disorderly one hundred square feet where he kept his journals, diaries, family albums, as well as old shoes, slippers, mementoes of his previous life. The rest of the house was overdone to his mind, all shine, and chandeliers. Too much white, too much neutrality. Even the couches were white leather. He was afraid to sit down. The dining table was steel and glass, hardly used, she rarely cooked. Damn it, she rarely ate. No curtains, only white blinds. Uncarpeted floors which in Glasgow during winter was not inviting, especially when the place cost an arm and a leg to heat.

He used to wonder why men had dens. His father's had been an old shed. He'd sit on a self-made bench and smoke, surrounded by shag tins full of sundry nails, screws, and the like. Ben could almost smell the shed now but, taking a slug of his lager, he realised that was probably a mix of hops and smelly socks.

When married to Siobhan, he hadn't needed a bolthole. How he wished Siobhan were still here with her soft voice and warm touch. Especially tonight on the eve of their youngest daughter's wedding.

Surely Gail would be on her best behaviour and not upset anyone too much. Why had he married this sharp-tongued vixen?

*

Saturday grew warmer by the hour and Ben sweated in his kilt, waistcoat, and high-collared shirt. Through the doors the shaded church promised a welcome coolness, but he was still in the sun-drenched courtyard with his daughter, Cara, waiting for the entrance hymn. It was a good match with Tom. But at this moment she was holding off tears and so was Ben.

'Try to remember Mum would be proud.'

'But I wish…'

'I know, sweetheart.' He hugged her as close as he could given the yards of silk and chiffon billowing between them.

As he walked his daughter up the aisle, he tried not to think about Gail waiting in the front pew. He was holding his breath but so far she'd been the model partner. Kind and considerate all morning, she'd even ironed his shirt, a menial task she always evaded.

After passing his daughter to her intended, he slipped in beside Gail. She smiled up at him and took his arm, hugging him to her so tight he was forced into a semi-reclining position. When he was sure she was focussed on the ceremony he levered himself up to a vertical angle and turned his head to her profile. Today, her face wasn't caked in make-up and her hair fell in a copper sweep down her back. She looked ahead in a kind of rapture, the locket gleaming between the hollow at her throat and the rise of her breasts.

He shook himself and turned to study his daughter kneeling at the altar. What if he let her down?

Had to admit he'd made a mistake, had to, God forbid, move in with her and her new husband until he could rent a flat. The others had children, there'd be no room.

His mind wandered back to the locket and to Granny Isla. After Gail's mother had died in childbirth, she'd brought her granddaughter up single handed, seen her through university and somehow got her started through contacts at the firm where she'd sailed through the ranks. He'd met Isla only twice, that once at the cottage out at Drymen, and then their wedding. She wasn't mad at all, but very astute, intelligence seeping through every pore, her green eyes dazzling under the piled-up grey hair. She'd said something he hadn't understood and let pass at the time but now it teased at his brain. What was it?

The organ blared and they stood up for the responsorial psalm, Gail turned and smiled at him so sweetly, he could only manage a nervous smile back. Her eyes were full of what looked suspiciously like desire.

The locket gleamed.

By the time they were through the vows, Gail was weeping quietly into her hanky, her arm entwined in his. When she turned to stare up at him her eyes were puffy, and mascara had dripped like wet ash down her cheeks. Should he tell her? She'd be furious. But she'd be equally furious if he let her walk into the full glare of the sun looking like that. He took his handkerchief from his waistcoat pocket, spat on it, and held her chin whilst he wiped away most of the mess.

She didn't resist but batted her eyelashes and murmured a rather meek, 'Thank you, darling.'

As the bells peeled congratulations, they filed out of the church and around the corner to the hall where the reception was to be held. Gail stopped to kiss the bride on her cheek and tell her how beautiful she looked. Ben was in a daze. Gail always complained that Cara needed to lose both the weight and the glasses.

They moved to their seats at the top table. Ben could hardly protest when Cara's new mother-in-law sat beside Gail, and they kissed cheeks like old friends. Ben smiled inanely, trying not to listen to their conversation. This was such a mismatch. Who put them together? Mrs McLean was a cleaner by profession, widowed, and tender bait for Gail. He oscillated between needing to check in and needing to not know what was being said. It seemed to be going okay until Gail invited the woman to accompany them on a cruise she was planning. Heck, they were all going. The honeymooners and Ben, as soon as 'her darling' could arrange time off from the hospital. He heard Gail say, 'It's my grandmother's inheritance. Wonderful woman. See, she left me this too. Isn't it divine?' She stretched her neck and ran her forefinger around the locket. 'I don't think I'll ever take it off.'

And then it came to him. After their stroll in the garden, with the scent of wild strawberries still lingering, the old lady had sat down on her wicker couch and watched Gail fuss with her car keys.

When Gail had gone to the bathroom, Isla had beckoned him, eyes hooded, fingers curled.

'Sit down beside me, Benjamin, my dear.'

When he sat gingerly on the edge of the seat, she shimmied up so close he could feel her thigh bones.

She fingered the hair away from his ear, sharp nails scratching at his scalp, and in a hoarse whisper said, 'She's a contradiction is my Gail. She'll be hard work, push you away, but don't give up on her. She's yet to find our soul. I'll ensure she does. Make up for spoiling her, making things too easy for her.'

The locket gleamed.

Raymond Jones

PLEA

Sit with me and hear why I cry within,
I am a stranger in your perfect world.
You are my flesh my blood please let me in,
let me join, let me watch your lives unfurl.
Let me share some days, no I won't intrude,
I will not impose any thoughts on you,
I will not dictate, please don't exclude,
my intention is not to dissolve your glue.
Give me reasons to make me stop trying,
give me reasons that makes me understand,
tell me why you're breeding this silence,
and why I'm destined to be second hand.

Is my punishment to square the circle?

My punishment is to square the circle.

Shirley Bell

Munchausen

It looks a bit like Munchausens by proxy
as three weeks in a row I've hurried in
to catch up with the ambulances and find out
how or if they are.

Twice it was my husband. This time
I found my mother dying in a chair. Paralysed
with pain, raging with infection and futile protests
that I've called three nines.

As if I could have left her, dry-mouthed,
with swollen legs patterned in weeping fractals.
Calling for my brother who is 132 miles away
in Surrey, not in this house.

Magpies

I am driving where the ambulance has driven
though much more quietly of course.
And, as I drive, I greet the magpies that I pass
and ask about their families. While rooks
arrange themselves in trees like books
on shelves.

At the hospital you are OK but
the woman in the next bed is not so lucky.
The heart care nurse, the trauma nurse
and several doctors are crowding round her X-ray.

And they are laughing - not maliciously -
in the way you laugh when actually you're shocked.
Apparently, it's a really odd aneurysm.
Like nothing they have ever seen before.

Brendan Magee

The Last Call

Characters

Seamus - 70s retired bricklayer terminally ill- London
Lisa - 20/30s trainee social worker
Clerk - Female working in 1970 Benefit Office in London
Maria - Female tango Dancer
Sean - Brother to Seamus Lives in Ireland/Donegal
Rose - sister-in-law to Seamus
Pauline - Pub landlady in London originally from Mayo
Vicky - counter clerk in bookies in London
Solicitor - Female solicitor in law firm in Ireland
Seamus' parents - Lived in Donegal
Policewoman - outside closed embassy in London

The Last Call is the story of Seamus Boyle an Irishman in his 70s living in a bedsit in London and who is terminally ill. He is visited by Lisa a trainee social worker. They explore his background in London and issues with his family in Ireland.

All the scenes are two handers aiming for the two actors to play the various roles.

(Exterior door to shabby bedsit. Young woman ringing door bell.)

Voice off stage:
Mr Boyle. Are you there?

(No reply)

Voice off stage:
Mr Boyle. I'm Lisa from Social Services. I want to come in for a chat.

Seamus:
You can go away. I'm still alive. Put that in your report.

Lisa:
But I just want to check things are OK.

(Lisa checks her phone for messages.)

Seamus:
They're great. Anyway, I've never heard of you. Who are you?

Lisa:
I'm Lisa. I'm a trainee social worker with central London social services.

Seamus:
No harm to you Lisa but feck off and come

back when you are qualified.

Lisa:
Please Mr Boyle just give me five minutes.

(The door is opened. Lisa walks in. Seamus is sitting on a bed.)

Seamus:
I suppose if I don't let you in, you'll only be back every day.

Lisa:
I'm only here to help. Your GP asked us to pop round.

Seamus:
Tell Doc Patel I'm still breathing. Anything else?

Lisa:
I want to talk about the future and help you plan it.

Interior farmhouse Ireland

Mother:
Are you happy now?

Father:
What?

Mother:
Packed his bag. Gone. You have what you wanted.

Father:
Ah to hell with him for all the good he's been.

Mother:
There's none as blind. You wouldn't still have a roof over your head if it wasn't for Seamus.

Father:
Well, am I not the lucky man? At least it's one less mouth to feed. I'm away to the bog meadow.

Door slams. Mother in tears.

INTERIOR LABOUR EXCHANGE - London

Clerk:
Yes. Name?

Seamus:
Seamus Boyle

Clerk:
Age?

Seamus:
Five.

Clerk:
What?

Seamus:
Five, I am a leap year baby.

Clerk:
Year of birth

Seamus:
1942.

Clerk:
Twenty-one then. Place of birth?

Seamus:
Donegal. Republic of Ireland.

Clerk:
What are you looking for? National Insurance number, Cards, Job?

Seamus:
All of them.

Clerk:
Qualifications?

Seamus:
Surviving ten years at the National School.

Clerk:
Experience, skills?

Seamus:
I can milk ten cows in thirty minutes. Fill a cart load of turf in ten minutes. Dance a four-hand reel on my own. Seamus get up to dance.

Clerk:
Sit down. Have you any health problems?

Seamus:
No.

Clerk:

Your countrymen have a contract on an office block in Westminster. The brickies are looking for hod carriers. Right?

Seamus:

OK when do I start, Monday?

Clerk:

No, now.

EXTERIOR: Dance Hall – Country and Irish music playing

Seamus:

Outside *(talking to himself)* - drink in hand

Come on you can do this. You've done it hundreds of times. Don't lose your bottle. Just see the Galtymore as a big parochial hall and loads of Irish.

I need another. No, you don't. Get in there with the best of them.

You've only been rejected once. Remember that was the American who'd got lost in Derry and you were half full.

In you go. Hundreds of women in there. Bound to be one to dance with you. Not everyone can jive. Go for a waltz.

(Seamus hears the waltz music start. He dries the palm of his hands on his trousers and heads for the door. He sees two bouncers, loses courage and walks back.)

INTERIOR: large kitchen part of a large house. Woman (Maria) foreign accent is teaching Seamus how to dance the Tango. She is expert. He has been improving.

Seamus:
I need to be getting back Maria. The boys will be moaning. We're only half way with the wall.

Maria:
OK. See you tomorrow. More steps.

Seamus:
I wish I could see you tonight.

Maria:
You know I'll be working tonight. The ambassador has a big party. I have to do the buffet.

(Maria kisses Seamus and gives him 2 bottles of beer.)

EXTERIOR door to a large house. Seamus arrives. A policewoman is standing on guard.

Policewoman:
Can I help you sir?

Seamus:
It's OK. I'm working here building a wall.

Policewoman:
Not today I'm afraid.

Seamus:
Why not?

Policewoman:
Have you not heard? The embassy is closed. There's been a coup. The staff have been recalled. They all flew home late last night or first thing this morning.

Seamus:
All?

Policewoman:
Everyone. You're not Seamus by any chance?

Seamus:
Yes.

Policewoman:
A woman left this note and a case of beer for you.

(Policewoman hands over letter and points him to case of beer.)

Interior bedsit: Seamus is sitting slumped in a chair surrounded by empties and letter lying on his chest. Tears and heartbreak. Sad song playing.

Interior pub London. Seamus, landlady Pauline

Seamus:
Pauline,any chance of a sub til Friday?

Pauline:
Not again Seamus. What do you do with it?

Seamus:
What do you think I do with it? Pay for your holiday in Spain every year.

Pauline:
Crossmolina when I go home to see my mother. That's what you should do.

Seamus:
What would be the point? My mother doesn't live in Crossmolina.

Pauline:

You're the smart one. Here twenty. I want it back on Friday. Where's your pub buddies this evening?

Pauline hands him a twenty-pound note…

Seamus:

Lenny' Mind the doors' will be counting the trains through Earls Court. Richard 'The Judge' will be issuing the sentences at least in his own mind. He's only an usher at the District Court, not the Crown Court.

Pauline:

What about Sylvia?

Seamus:

I'm sorry she's not in.

Pauline:

Do you fancy her?

Seamus:

Yeah, for a pint. God her old man left her well off.

INTERIOR PUB IRELAND early 1970s

(Seamus and Rose (his sister-in-law) sitting at a table.)

Rose:
A sad time.

Seamus:
I've had worse.

Rose:
Sean is very upset.

Seamus:
Well, Da thought more of him than he ever thought of me. Where is Sean anyway?

Rose:
He's just sorting out a few things.

Seamus:
At the solicitors I suppose.

Rose:
Oh no, sure there's no will anyway. The farm will be between the pair of you. Not that it's worth much. Bad land and Sean had to put a few thousand into getting the home place done up. But you must be doing alright with bricklaying in London. They say there's good money in it.

Seamus:
It's a living. Are you trying to ask me for a contribution for the funeral costs.

Rose:
Oh no,no. Mind you it's not cheap when you pay the undertaker, the priest and give a few quid to the gravediggers.

(Seamus taking notes from his pocket.)

Seamus:
Here take this.

Rose:
No, Sean would never accept any money... Have you ever thought of coming back home to Ireland.

Seamus:
There's nothing to come back for. My home is in London now.

Rose:
What about the farm? Sean has put a lot into it to keep it going.

Seamus:
What about it. I always hated it.

Rose:
Well Sean has his heart in it.

Seamus:
Good for him. He can do what he likes with it.

Rose:
Sure, it's hardly worth anything. There's more debt than money in it. So can I tell the solicitor you have no interest in it.

Seamus:
Yeah.

Rose:
Look just sign this beermat. I'll get Eugene the barman to witness it. Another pint of Guinness? A packet of crisps?

INTERIOR: Bedsit

Lisa:
So, you gave your share of the farm for a pint and a packet of crisps.

Seamus:
Aye. And salt and vinegar at that. I hate salt and vinegar crisps.

Lisa:
I can see that would make you bitter. Do you have any savings? I want to see what support we can arrange for you.

Seamus:
I have no savings but that's not what has really pissed me off.

INTERIOR CAR

(Seamus in car with Rose driving.)

Seamus:
Nice car. What make is it?

Rose:
A BMW. Very comfortable isn't it?

Seamus:
Certainly, better than a bike or pony and trap.

Rose:
I prefer the Merc myself but Sean's using it today.

Seamus:
You must be doing well two cars.

Rose:
Can't complain but it's pressure, pressure.

Seamus:
I'm surprised that Sean didn't collect me but I suppose he is sorting out the funeral arrangements

Rose:
He's seeing the bank manager. The housing development is at final contract stage so he just had a loan arrangement to sign with this morning. It's sad about your mother, she died quickly in the end.

Seamus:
It comes to us all but she was a great woman. She had a hard life I don't know how she ever put up with the auld fella.

Rose:
It was tough in the beginning. But she was happy in the recent years on her own and with a bit of money. She often talked of you Seamus. She missed you and wondered why you never came to see her.

Seamus:
Well, I used to ring and send the odd card. Things weren't always easy for me. Anyway what 's the building Sean's getting the money for?

Rose:
He's building fourteen houses in the bog meadow.

Seamus:
Are they houseboats? Sure, that field is a swamp.

Rose:
Not really. He's put in a few drains. Anyway what about yourself Me and Sean often wonder why you never bought your place in London. I believe you can buy your Council flat at a good discount.

Seamus:
With what, fresh air. The back will only last so long on the bricklaying.

Rose:
Sean would have given you the money.

Seamus:
As long as I put it in his name.

Rose:
Sean 's not like that. He'd only want to help you.

Seamus:
In the same way he helped himself to the farm.

Rose:

That's not true. You let him have it. Wasn't it almost a ruin when he took it over. He took a big chance. He wasn't to know that joining the EU would improve the value of land and then the Celtic tiger.

Seamus:

Well, he tamed the beast.

INTERIOR: Bedsit - Seamus and Lisa.

Lisa:

So can I take it he never shared anything with you.

Seamus:

He wouldn't give you the snot from his nose.

Lisa:

What is your financial position? I assume you have the state pension. Do you have any other pension or savings?

Seamus:

Well at the last count I have eighteen pounds and twenty six pence.

Lisa:

Are you receiving any other benefits? Attendance allowance?

Seamus:

No.

Lisa:

With your illness you would qualify for Attendance allowance. In fact, you might qualify for backdating of the allowance as you been ill for so long. I'll also look at caring arrangements. You might be able to get a half an hour a day.

Seamus:

As much as that. Thanks anyway and I'm sorry I was narky when you arrived. It's the pain and I'm out of Powers. Do you want an arrowroot?

Lisa:

No thanks. I'm late for my next call. Do you mind if I write you up as a case study for my finals thesis.

Seamus:

If you want.

Lisa:

See you soon.

INTERIOR: Bookies shop
(Seamus and Vicky – cashier/counter clerk in Bookies Seamus at the counter.)

Vicky:
Wow that was some win Seamus. You've nearly bankrupt us. What a double. Who gave you the tip.

Seamus:
The Social Security

(Vicky starts counting out the money.)

Vicky:
We haven't seen you for a while. How have you been keeping?

Seamus:
Well, I can still wipe my own arse.

Vicky:
I hope you have washed your hands before you filled in the docket… What are you going to do with all this money. A world cruise?

Seamus:
I might have a trip down the Thames.

Vicky:
You know how to live it up.

(Seamus hands Vicky a fifty pound note.)

Seamus:
Have a bicardi on me.

INTERIOR Solicitors office.

(Sean (Seamus's brother) and female solicitor)

Solicitor:
Thanks for coming in Sean. I am very sorry to hear about Seamus. I'm sure it was very upsetting for you.

Sean:
It was sad but we were expecting it. A social worker in London had been in touch to tell us he was ill. But you know what it's like with all the pressure, I wasn't able to get over to see him before he died.

Solicitor:
I can understand. I've invited you in because Seamus's solicitors in London have contacted us and asked us to sort out a few things at this end.

Sean:
I'm not having to pay for his funeral am I?

Solicitor:
Oh no. I've got a copy of his will. He's left quite a bit of money.

Sean:

That's a surprise I didn't think he had a penny. He had a hard life. He was a grafter. I was always on to him to move back here and retire. Me and the wife would have looked after him.

Solicitor:

He has left a few small bequests and to you Sean ten Euro for a pint of Guinness and a packet of crisps, Salt and Vinegar. He's also left you a property to share here.

Sean:

I didn't know he owned a property in Ireland.

Solicitor:

Well, he's just having it built. I've spoken to the builders and they said it would be ready in two months.

Sean:

That's quick for a house.

Solicitor:

It's a house of sorts. It's a mausoleum. You to share.

The End

Polly Richardson

Dingle Wilds 37 Wind Catchers

Salty sea droplets deposits decorate roughened cheeks
peering to sun beams bulging though heavy dull veil
scudding west chasing south,
as if precious laborious moments of new-borns head in vulva
trying
to birth. Both moments equally momentous, both moments
two branches of viable existence,
continuity and bloom. Sun. Life. New.
Gusts announced themselves anonymously, as they do
here, this place. The gull in flight moves nowhere, flocks below
balk eye up flight in vain,
nestle with sand. I heard the clams sing to plumes beneath wild
roars.
I'm rooted.

unlike rain dances across coastal juts, it sways
mirroring rising waves, arriving plops ripples awaiting pools
matching my eyes, horizons higher than moon sending itself
plunging to shore
wind catcher surfs white crests, hands to kite - bold, bright,
scooping squall. He scuds south chasing west disappears,
reappears, head between rolls skimming surface. Hours,
seconds moments whossssh - flight quick yet slow, time
stopped. Surfing air, board to stars. He flew. Minuets, moments
momentous, as swan lands with grace catching wind. Beams
bulged through. Branches of viable existence

Dingle wilds 39 Solitude part 3

Stilling with solitude, the gift. Beautiful. Bold. Raw. Paints harmoniously as if on blank canvas

creating its own masterpiece with silence, silence within - birthing as if newborn

First ponderous look at mother's whispers dancing themselves to heartbeats in tandem. Solitude.

Precious moments branching into every capillary flowing infinitely, beyond breath.

And nature's bursting joy sings out marvelously. I imagine oceanic moments, her rolling white horses galloping to graze shores, prancing breathless at first touch to sands kissed by sun. Solitude...

When mist blankets, and breeze blows encompassing joy where birds play and sea sprays lands last deposits from her surge as a reminder life buds even in the most rugged of places, blooming brilliant, wilding rainbows rooted, stilling with solitude, the gift. Beautiful. Bold. Raw. Do you dare to reach beyond your walls and walk completely bare, beautiful. Bold. Raw. Solitary.

About the Authors

Howard Debs (Page 14)

Howard Richard Debs is a recipient of the 2015 Anna Davidson Rosenberg Poetry Awards. His essays, fiction, and poetry appear internationally in numerous publications; His book Gallery: A Collection of Pictures and Words is a 2017 Best Book Awards and 2018 Book Excellence Awards recipient. His chapbook Political is the 2021 American Writing Awards winner in poetry. He is co-editor of New Voices: Contemporary Writers Confronting the Holocaust forthcoming from Vallentine Mitchell of London, publisher of the first English language edition of Anne Frank's diary. He is listed in the Poets & Writers Directory.

Danny Best (Page 16)

I'm a retired cook, then truck driver, now poet & actor. I see poetry as an opportunity to communicate and connect with all kindred spirits in a way that may offer good practical food for thought, but also in ways that will encourage readers to go beyond their own normal comfort zones and explore other subject matter they may not have previously considered.

I usually write from memories of my own personal life lessons or I simply try to tap into what my dreams leave lingering within my disheveled pillow cases. Forever hopeful to convey all such experiences with the reader/s. Lists of my literary credits will be made available upon request.

Mark Blickley (Page 18)

Mark Blickley grew up within walking distance of New York's Bronx Zoo and is a proud member of the Dramatists Guild and PEN American Center. He is the recipient of a MacArthur Foundation Scholarship Award for Drama and author of the story collection Sacred Misfits (Red Hen Press, Los Angeles). His multi-genre collaborations with artist Amy Bassin include Weathered Reports: Trump Surrogate Quotes from the Underground (Moira Books, Chicago) and the text-based art book Dream Streams (Clare Songbirds Publishing House, New York). His latest book is the flash fiction collection Hunger Pains (Buttonhook Press).

Margaret Royall (Page 22)

Margaret Royall has five books of poetry and a memoir published. She has appeared widely in print, online and poetry anthologies, has won/been short-listed in several competitions and her collection 'Where Flora Sings', published by Hedgehog Press, was nominated for the Laurel Prize in 2021. Her latest collection, 'Immersed in Blue' was published January 2022 by Impspired Press. She leads a women's poetry group in Nottinghamshire and performs open mic sessions online and in person. She is currently working on a third poetry collection.
Website: https://margaretroyall.com/
Twitter:@RoyallMargaret Instagram: meggiepoet

Susie Gharib (Page 31)

Susie Gharib undertook postgraduate studies at the University of Strathclyde in Glasgow. Her doctoral thesis is on the work of D.H. Lawrence. Classical Adaptations (2002), her first published book, consists of adaptations of Charlotte Bronte's Villette, Virginia Woolf's The Waves, and D.H. Lawrence's Lady Chatterley's Lover. Her poetry, fiction, literary essays, and film reviews have been published in almost fifty literary magazines and journals.

J.S Watts (Page 34)

J.S.Watts is a poet and novelist whose writing appears in publications in Britain and abroad and has been broadcast on BBC and Independent Radio. She has published eight books: two poetry collections, "Cats and Other Myths" and " Years Ago You Coloured Me", plus multi-award nominated SF poetry pamphlet, "Songs of Steelyard Sue" (Lapwing Publications) and her most recent pamphlet, "The Submerged Sea" (Dempsey & Windle), also four novels, "A Darker Moon" - dark literary fantasy, and "Witchlight", "Old Light" and "Elderlight"- paranormal (Vagabondage Press). See www.jswatts.co.uk for further details.

Sherry Shahan (Page 35)

Sherry Shahan watches the world from behind; whether in the hub of Oxford, an alley in Havana, or alone in a squat hotel room in Paris; whether with a 35 mm camera or an iPhone. Her photographs have appeared in The Los Angeles Times, San Francisco Chronicle, Fourth River,

Gargoyle, Montana Mouthful, Literary Mama and elsewhere. She holds an MFA from Vermont College of Fine Arts and taught a creative writing class for UCLA Extension for 10 years.

Douglas Colston (Page 39)

Douglas Colston has played in Ska bands, picked up university degrees, supported his parents during terminal illnesses, married his love, fathered two great children, had his inheritance embezzled, transitioned into Counselling as a vocation and experienced debilitating mental and physical illnesses. Now, among other things, he is pursuing a PhD.

RP Verlaine (Page 41)

Rp Verlaine lives in New York City.
He has an MFA in creative writing from City College.
He taught in New York Public schools for many years.
His first volume of poetry- Damaged by Dames & Drinking was published in 2017 and another – Femme Fatales Movie Starlets & Rockers in 2018. A set of three e-books titled Lies From The Autobiography vol 1-3 were published from 2018 to 2020. His newest book, Imagined Indecencies, was published in February of 2022.

James Mulhern (Page 43)

James Mulhern's writing has appeared in literary journals over two hundred times and has received many awards. Mr. Mulhern was granted a writing fellowship to Oxford University. A short story was longlisted for the Fish Short Story Prize. In 2017, he was nominated for a Pushcart Prize. His novel, Give Them Unquiet Dreams, is a Kirkus Reviews Best Book of the Year. He was shortlisted for the Aesthetica Creative Writing Award 2021 for his poetry.

Jim Bates (Page 79)

Jim lives in a small-town twenty miles west of Minneapolis, Minnesota. His stories and poems have appeared in over three hundred publications. "Resilience" a collection of twenty-seven short stories was published by Bridge House Publishing. "Periodic Stories" and "Periodic Stories Volume Two" were published by Impspired. A dystopian adventure novella "Something Better" was published by Dark Myth Publications. "Short Stuff" a collection of flash fiction and drabbles was published by Chapeltown Books. His story "Aliens" was nominated for the 2020 Pushcart Prize. His story "The Maple Leaf" was selected Non-Poetic Publication of the year by the readers of Spillwords. www.theviewfromlonglake.wordpress.com.

Jyoti Nair (Page 84)

Intrinsically from career per se, as an L&D professional spearheading numerous business units in the HR compass, Jyoti Nair is quite intrigued, with respect to the human behavior spectrum, its layered richness, and uncanny complexities. Ms. Nair has recently adopted a nom de plume as 'Aarya', her works have found havens in distinguished poetry journals. She has won some key accolades in the literary landscape, such as, The Certificate of Excellence by English Poets, Literary Excellence Certificate by Gujarat Sahitya Academy, to name a few. She envisages dawns where her poetry could be mobilized as indomitable propellers, to accelerate the eradication of blatant social evils.

John Welsh (Page 85)

My name is John and I am an addict
It started in my youth, the cravings that started to invade my thoughts made me reclusive and I would retire to my bedroom. I could not get enough of them back then and I have tried and failed many times to cure this.
The need intensified and I was regularly found loitering around book and stationery outlets with a wallet full of loyalty cards. The addiction always grows. What was just word fix accelerated into phrases, sentences, poems, paragraphs and chapters.
I did a few lines last night (personal use only)
Yes, my name is John and I am a wordaholic.

Ann Christine Tabaka (Page 86)

Ann Christine Tabaka was nominated for the 2017 Pushcart Prize in Poetry. She is the winner of Spillwords Press 2020 Publication of the Year, her bio is featured in the "Who's Who of Emerging Writers 2020 and 2021," published by Sweetycat Press. She is the author of 14 poetry books, and 1 short story book. She lives in Delaware, USA. She loves gardening and cooking. Chris lives with her husband and four cats. Her most recent credits are: Eclipse Lit, Carolina Muse, Sparks of Calliope; The Closed Eye Open, North Dakota Quarterly, Tangled Locks Journal, Wild Roof Journal, The American Writers Review.

Peter Magliocco (Page 87)

Peter Magliocco writes from Las Vegas, Nevada, where he's been active as poet, writer, artist, and editor of ART: MAG for several years. A multiple Best of the Net and Pushcart Press nominee, he has recent poetry at LOTHLORIEN POETRY JOURNAL, IMPSPIRED, TROUVAILLE REVIEW, DREICH, TAJ MAHAL REVIEW, FLASHES OF BRILLIANCE, and elsewhere. His latest poetry books are The Underground Movie Poems (Horror Sleaze Trash), Night Pictures from the Climate Change (Cyberwit.net), and Particle Acceleration on Judgement Day (Impspired). His recent sci-fi horror novel, Eye of Aliena, is available at Amazon.

DC Diamondopolous (Page 92)

DC Diamondopolous is an award-winning short story, and flash fiction writer with hundreds of stories published internationally in print and online magazines, literary journals, and anthologies. DC's stories have appeared in: Progenitor, 34th Parallel, So It Goes: The Literary Journal of the Kurt Vonnegut Museum and Library, Lunch Ticket, and others. DC's recently released collection Captured Up Close (20th Century Short-Short Stories) has two Pushcart Prize nominated stories and one nominated for Best of the Net Anthology. Her first collection of stories was Stepping Up. She lives on the California coast with her wife and animals. dcdiamondopolous.com

Sarah Mackey Kirby (Page 100)

Sarah Mackey Kirby grew up in Louisville, Kentucky. She is the author of the poetry collection, The Taste of Your Music (Impspired, 2021). Her poems appear in Impspired Magazine, Muddy River Poetry Review, Ploughshares, Third Wednesday, The New Verse News, and elsewhere. She and her husband spend their time in Kentucky and Ohio. https://smkirby.com/

Linda Imbler (Page 105)

Linda Imbler's poetry collections include six published paperbacks: Big Questions, Little Sleep, Big Questions, Little Sleep" second edition, Lost and Found, Red Is The Sunrise, Bus Lights, Travel Sights, and Spica's Frequency. Soma Publishing has published her four e-book collections, The Sea's Secret Song, Pairings-a hybrid of short fiction and poetry, That Fifth Element, and Per Quindecim. Her next publication from Soma Publishing titled Rhythms Told is coming in late Autumn. Linda has been nominated for one Pushcart Prize and six Best of the Nets. Examples of her poetry and a listing of publications can be found at lindaspoetryblog.blogspot.com.

Lisa 'Annie' Harpel (Page 108)

Annie Harpel lives in a quiet beach town along the Central Coast of California, and finds inspiration for much of her writing in her surroundings. She is a poet, poetry teacher, essayist, artist and fine art photographer. Her debut book of poetry, "The Blue Hour" was published by Impspired Dec. 2022.

Ken Cathers (Page 110)

Ken was born (1951) and raised in Ladysmith on Vancouver Island. He has a B.A. from the University of Victoria and a M.A. from York University in Toronto. He has also been published in numerous periodicals, over 12 anthologies as well as seven books of poetry, most recently Letters From the Old Country with Ekstasis Press. Ken lives in the country with his family and his trees.

He has recently had work published in Impspired, The MacGuffin, Bluebird Word, Zoetic press and have writing forthcoming in the Remington Review and a chapbook from broke press in B.C. Canada.

David Milner (Page 111)

David's stories have appeared in Duality Books, Friday Flash Fiction, Spillwords Press and performed on Resonance FM radio (UK). He was commissioned to adapt and direct his short story 'Into The Breach' for the 2021 Rise of the Resistance festival, screened at Bloomsbury Theatre London, Wellcome Collection and available online. For several years he worked in the public sector, mostly with homeless charities. David was a founder member of punk band Vee V V (Edils Records). He finds his stories while he's out and about, or they find him… He lives with his wife and family in London.

Janice Mathis (Page 117)

Janice Mathis lives in Acworth, GA with her husband of 37 years. She works as a Medical Assistant for a private Physician group. Janice has always enjoyed music and poetry, but has only begun to seriously pursue writing in recent years. Using writing as an emotional outlet, she finds inspiration in the beauty of nature, the dynamics of relationships and love of her family.

She has a self-published collection of poems, and has been published by Alien Buddha Press, Impspired, and Sweetycat Press. Her second collection, 'Broken Bits for the Mosaic', has recently been released by Alien Buddha Press.

Kathleen Denizard (Page 121)

I am a former teacher of English and for many years worked in social services addressing the needs of residents in affordable housing.
There is pure joy for me in sharing my poetry and other writing, in relating the many wonders of life and human experiences as a mature observer of people and nature. Living on the seacoast in Massachusetts has significant influence in my writing endeavors. It is the "feel" and beauty of language, too, that inspires me to set my thoughts into words sincerely and universally.

Charlie Brice (Page 124)

Charlie Brice won the 2020 Field Guide Poetry Magazine Poetry Contest and placed third in the 2021 Allen Ginsberg Poetry Prize. His fifth full-length poetry collection is The Ventriloquist (WordTech Editions, 2022). His poetry has been nominated twice for the Best of Net Anthology and three times for a Pushcart Prize and has appeared in Atlanta Review, The Honest Ulsterman, Ibbetson Street, The Paterson Literary Review, Impspired Magazine, Muddy River Poetry Review, and elsewhere.

Robbie Taylor (Page 126)

I came to writing through therapy at age forty-eight, and, nearly ten years later, I still need it. Writing I mean. We find things in life, that are not so bad sometimes and in that discovery, we find ourselves a little, and another jigsaw piece is slotted home. Writing has also proved to me, that its the pieces that are lost that complete the picture of who we really are. There is a little bit of me in everything I write, not blood, not flesh maybe, but the bit that accepts that just because a piece of sky is missing, it doesn't mean the rest will collapse around me.

Mehreen Ahmed (Page 131)

Multiple contests winner for short fiction, Mehreen Ahmed is an Australian novelist born in Bangladesh. Her historical fiction, The Pacifist, is a Drunken Druid's Editor's Choice and an Amazon Audible bestseller. Gatherings is nominated for the James Tait Black Prize for fiction. Her flash-micro fictions have also been nominated for 3xbotN, Pushcart.

L.B Sedlacek (Page 133)

LB Sedlacek has had poems and stories appear in a variety of journals and zines.
Her latest fiction book is "The Jackalope Committee and Other Tales" published by Alien Buddha Press. Her poetry books include "Swim," "I'm No Robot," "The Poet Next Door," "Simultaneous Submissions," "Happy Little Clouds," and "Words and Bones." LB also likes to swim and read.

Ken Weene (Page 150)
With a Ph.D. in psychology and a never-ending love for language, writing, and his fellow humans, Kenneth Weene has devoted the past twenty years to creating stories, poems, essays, novels, and plays, many of which are available on Amazon and on Ken's website www.kennethweene.com

Keith E. Sparks Jr (Page 151)
Keith E. Sparks Jr. has been published in various literary venues and has been nominated for the Pushcart Poetry Prize. He has published multiple collections of poetry and was the creator and former editor of Open Skies Quarterly. Keith resides in West Virginia with his wife and three children whom are the epicenter of his existence.

Lisa White (Page 154)
Lisa White has been writing since around 9 years old. She writes on many subjects, but her favorites are regarding nature and love. Married, her wife and 3 kids give her many sources of inspiration. Her work has appeared in various anthologies and she is currently in the process of working on a small poetry collection to be released in 2022. For more information and a deeper glimpse into her work you can follow Lisa on her Facebook page "Me, Myself and Insanity."

Maggie MacKay (Page 156)

Maggie Mackay's pamphlet 'The Heart of the Run,' Picaroon Poetry, 2018 was followed by her full collection 'A West Coast Psalter', Kelsay Books, 2021. In 2020 she was awarded a place in the Poetry Archive's WordView permanent collection. She reviews poetry pamphlets at https://sphinxreview.co.uk (Happenstance Press) and collections at The Friday Poem (https://thefridaypoem.com).She can be found on Twitter @Bonniedreamer.

Dorthy LaVern Spencer McCarthy(Page 158)

LaVern Spencer McCarthy has written and published nine books, five of poetry and four of fiction.
Her work has appeared in Writers and Readers Magazine, Meadowlark Reader, Agape Review, Fenechty Publications Anthologies Of Short Stories, From The Shadows, An Anthology Of Short Stories, Visions International, Fresh Words International Magazine and others. She is a life member of The Poetry Society Of Texas and National Federation of State Poetry Societies, Inc.
She resides in Blair Oklahoma where she is currently writing her fifth book of short stories.

Andrew Scott (Page 160)

Andrew Scott is a native of Fredericton, NB. During his time as an active poet, Andrew Scott has taken the time to speak in front of classrooms, judge poetry competitions, and have over 200 hundred writings published worldwide in such publications as The Art of Being Human, Battered Shadows and The Broken Ones.

Andrew Scott has published multiple poetry books, Snake with A Flower, The Phoenix Has Risen, The Path, The Storm Is Coming, Whispers of the Calm, Searching and Letter To You and one book of photography, Through My Eyes. Redemption Avenue is his first novella

To contact Andrew,
email …andrewscott.scott@gmail.com
http://twitter.com/JustMaritimeBoy
http://andrewmscott.com
http://www.facebook.com/andymscott
http://www.facebook.com/JustaMaritimeBoy

Johanne Lee (Page 162)

Johanne Lee is a proud mother of 3 and Mancunian, presently published in 9 anthologies including Open Skies and The Sacred Feminine anthology to name a couple. Recently published By Impspired magazine. She is also a children's picture book author of Dream Big Little One, Maximus the Humpback Whale and Maison Mouse (all on Amazon) all of her books raise for charity. She is about to publish her own poetry Book, 'Womans Journey 'which will raise for Crossroads Derbyshire and can be found as Johanne Lee Author on FB and Instagram as well as joleeinpoetry on Instagram

Michael Minassian (Page 164)

MICHAEL MINASSIAN is a Contributing Editor for Verse-Virtual, an online poetry journal. His poetry collections Time is Not a River, Morning Calm, and A Matter of Timing are all available on Amazon. A new chapbook, Jack Pays a Visit, was released in 2022. For more information: https://michaelminassian.com

Victor Schwartzman (Page 166)

Victor Schwartzman, 76, was born in Brooklyn. He started writing when he was eight. He moved to Canada in 1968 (Vietnam War) and eventually became a Human Rights Officer for 23 years. He's terrible at submitting and only recently began sending out his stuff in earnest, or if not Earnest, Surely, and don't call him that. Victor's tried writing most everything but has the most satisfaction with flash fiction. His starting point on each story is: what is really important to me today? Publishing credits include The American Drivel Review!

Mauela Palacios (Page 169)

Manuela Palacios lectures on anglophone literature at the University of Santiago de Compostela (Galicia, Spain). She has edited, translated and written about Irish, Galician and Arabic poetry. Among the recent anthologies she has edited are Migrant Shores: Irish, Moroccan & Galician Poetry (Salmon Poetry 2017) and Ανθολογία Νέων Γαλικιανών Ποιητών - Antoloxía De Poesía Galega Nova (Vakxikon 2019). Manuela's research on women's studies, ecopoetry and the human-animal trope has set her on the stimulating path to creative writing.

Melissa Mulvihill (Page 171)

Melissa writes poetry, creative non-fiction, and fiction that explore themes related to impermanence, family relationships, and living with progressive illness. Her first chapbook, Something You Don't Know Yet, is forthcoming with ShadbAweg Press. You can find her at Melissamulvihill.com.

Calan McCarthy (Page 174)

Calan McCarthy is a writer of Irish descent who has written three novels, four short stories, and a collection of poems. His material covers multi-genres – Westerns, Spy, Science Fiction and Gothic. His three-part violent Western story Capstone is included in preceding editions of Impspired Literary Magazine. His most recent publication Stalemate is a Cold War spy novel penned as John Isaac.

Robin Holmes (Page 189)

Robin Holmes believes that growing up on a small hill farm in the Mourne Mountains in Northern Ireland has been a deeply formative experience for his writing. In his poetry he explores themes of the natural world, the life of birds, the changing seasons and man's problematic relationship to the environment. His work has appeared regularly in the Bangor Literary Journal and the annual Community Arts Partnership Poetry in Motion Journal.

Sinead Coxhill (Page 192)

Living by the sea in Northern Ireland, Sinead Coxhill's poetry is often inspired by the sea and coastal landscape. In 2019 she performed at the Red Sails and Stendhal Festivals in Northern Ireland, and at various Open Mic events in England. Her poems have been published in 4 anthologies: 'Spindrift', Portrush Writers, 2018, 'Heartland', CAP 2020, 'Reeling In', Portrush Writers, 2021, and 'Irish Hares and Seahorses', North Coast Writers, 2022.

Yvonne Hamilton (Page 194)

Yvonne Hamilton is a retired Primary School Teacher, living in the coastal town of Portstewart in Northern Ireland. She has been writing with North Coast Writers for three years now. Writing mainly serial prose and short stories, she also writes memoir pieces and poetry.

Mary Farrell (Page 197)

Mary Farrell, Facilitator of North Coast Writers in Northern Ireland, has been writing for five years, some poetry but she prefers writing short stories and Flash Fiction, particularly about human dynamics. Her Collections 'It's like Walking a Tightrope' and 'Out of the Chrysalis' were published by Impspired Press in 2021 and 2022.

Orla McFaul (Page 199)

Living in Northern Ireland with her family, Orla McFaul joined North Coast Writers in 2021. She is drawn to poetry, finding it cathartic and inspirational. She read two poems 'Twilight' and 'Changing Focus' at the Seamus Heaney Homeplace in Northern Ireland in 2021. Her poems are published in a Seamus Heaney Homeplace Pamphlet, ed Jessica Traynor, and in the Irish Hares and Seahorses Anthology, Impspired Press, both in 2022.

Gerladine Fleming (Page 201)

Geraldine Fleming retired early due to ill health. Drawn back into creative writing she found a supportive community when she joined North Coast Writers Group in Northern Ireland. She enjoys writing poetry and prose and has published in a number of journals, magazines and anthologies. She loves to write.

Ian Turnbull (Page 210)

Retired in Northern Ireland, Ian has been published in periodicals in both the US and the UK. He also devises improvised comedy sketches which are not scripted. He wrote scripts for videos whilst working for a television company, but it was on accounting. He is inspired by Christianity, where he lives and anything that isn't accounting.

Sue Steging (Page 211)

Sue Steging was born in Liverpool and now lives in rural Northern Ireland. She began writing in 2018, mostly poetry, mostly about the world around her, her efforts generously supported and encouraged by family, friends and local writers' networks. Some of her work has been published in journals and anthologies.

Emma E Kane (Page 213)

Living beside the sea in Northern Ireland with her partner and youngest child, Emma E. Kane is an avid ocean dipper often finding inspiration in the wild Atlantic. Her short story The Memory Tree was published in On the Grass When I Arrive, Guildhall Press, 2016. She is affiliated with North Coast Writers.

Paul Girvan (Page 214)

Paul Girvan is a recent member of North Coast Writers and lives on the North coast of Northern Ireland. A retired judge and formerly a senior barrister he delivered many written judgments and wrote extensively on legal matters over a career of fifty years but now enjoys the freedom of creative writing, particularly poetry, often inspired by his travels and by nature.

Mae Gardiner (Page 218)

Living on the North Coast of Ireland, Mae Gardiner draws inspiration from the people and places around her. She writes children's fairy tales, poetry, short stories and also paints. Having performed at Atlantic Craft NI Events throughout Ireland, her 'A Coat of Many Colours', 2020, is available on YouTube. Many of her poems were first published in three anthologies from Portrush Writers Group, Beachcombing 2014, Spindrift 2018, Reeling In' 2021.

Helen Hand (Page 222)

Helen Hand, a rogue Scot living in Dublin, is a retired IT Professional and although computer savvy she prefers to write with a pen. Always having written, she loves words and the surprises that appear when the ink hits the page. Her prose and poems feature in Pen to Paper, an anthology by Lucan Creative Writers, 2016, and in a Chapbook produced by Tallaght Library, 2021

Janet Peace (Page 223)

Janet Peace is a retired teacher living near the spectacular North Coast of Northern Ireland. Writing has been a comparatively new passion joyfully discovered since joining the North Coast Writers creative writing group., Her large family, many pets, the beauty that surrounds her and reflections on life all inspire her poetry.

Brenda McAteer (Page 225)

Brenda McAteer has been a member of North Coast Writers group for three years, enjoys writing short prose pieces, some included in the Anthology, 'Irish Hares and Seahorses', published by Impspired Press, 2022

Jimmy Milliken (Page 231)

Jimmy Milliken, member of North Coast Writers, writes poetry, taking inspiration from the natural world. Twice shortlisted for the Seamus Heaney Poetry Award; in 2018 and in 2020, his poems have been published in several anthologies. His collection "Cracking the air" will be published by Impspired Press this autumn.

Rhona Stephens (Page 232)

Born in Northern Ireland, Rhona Stephens has lived in each of the four nations of the United Kingdom. She divides her time between Royal Deeside in Scotland and the Causeway Coast of Northern Ireland. Joining North Coast Writers Group in September 2020, she has found fellow travelers who share her delight in unveiling the power, potential and pleasures of the written word.

Jane Avery (Page 235)

Jane Avery is a Poet from Kent. Along with work published in several Anthologies, she regularly contributes to The Open University Poets quarterly magazine. She is currently enrolled at West Dean College, formerly the home of the poet and patron of the arts Edward James. Here she hopes to achieve her Masters in Creative Writing and Publishing.

Chris Butler (Page 236)

Chris Butler is an illiterate poet howling from the Quiet Corner of Connecticut. His most recent chapbook of poems of pain, "DOOMER", was published by Ethel. He is currently working on his next collection of poems, "Antichris". He is also the co-editor of The Beatnik Cowboy.

Philip Dunkerley (Page 238)

Philip Dunkerley performs at open-mic and other events in South Lincolnshire, where he lives. He has run local poetry groups for a number of years, including the Stamford Stanza. His poems have appeared in a wide range of journals, webzines and anthologies, including Poetry Salzburg Review, Magma, Dream Catcher, Acumen, Impspired, IS&T, Lighten Up Online and Poems for Peace. He is a reviewer for Orbis.

David Congalton (Page 240)

David Congalton is a writer and radio host in San Luis Obispo, California. A former newspaper columnist, Congalton is the author of four nonfiction books, including "Man About Town: Stories of San Luis Obispo." He wrote the 2014 romantic comedy "Authors Anonymous," which starred Kaley Cuoco, Chris Klein, and Dennis Farina. Congalton currently serves on the faculty of the Rocaberti Screenwriters Retreat in Barcelona. His website is davecongaltonstories.com.

Mihaela Melnic (Page 244)

Mihaela Melnic is the author of the bilingual poetry collection "Change of Seasons" and co-author of the book "Evermore". She lives and writes in Rome, Italy where her prose and poetry evolve and take different shapes with every new life experience.

Her work has appeared in various anthologies and literary venues

including Dissident Voice, Poetica Review, Spillwords magazine, Mad Swirl, Lothlorien Poetry journal, Ariel Chart journal and The Piker Press.

For more of Melnic's published work visit her website: https://telluricverse.wordpress.com

Hillary Griffin (Page 246)

Hillary is a retired tax advisor. She started writing short stories and diaries during the summer of 2020 to reflect on the experiences of lockdown. Her other hobbies include running a Beaver Scout colony, learning to play the organ, Park Running and allotment gardening. Hillary lives on the Sefton coast and is married with two sons.

Eric Robert Nolan (Page 252)

Eric Robert Nolan's writing has appeared throughout over 50 publications in the United States, Canada, Britain, Ireland, Germany, Romania, Turkey, India and Australia. His work was also selected for ten anthologies, two chapbooks and six mini-books between 2013 and 2021. He was nominated for the Sundress Publications 2018

Best of the Net Anthology, and for Spillwords Press awards in 2020, 2021 and 2022. His debut novel was The Dogs Don't Bark in Brooklyn Any More, published in 2013 by Dagda Publishing in the United Kingdom. He is a past editor for the dystopian literature journal, The Bees Are Dead.

Sultana Raza (Page 254)

Of Indian origin, Sultana Raza's poems/fiction have appeared in 100+ journals. SFF work: Entropy, Columbia Journal, Star*line, Bewildering Stories, Focus & Vector (BSFA), Unlikely Stories Mark V, Galaxy#2 #4, #5, Antipodean SF, and File770.
Her fiction received an Honorable Mention in Glimmer Train Review. Also published in Coldnoon Journal, Knot Literature, and Setu. She's read her fiction/poems in Switzerland, France, Luxembourg, England, Ireland, the USA, WorldCon 2018, and CoNZealand 2019.
Her creative non-fiction has appeared in Literary Ladies Guide, Literary Yard, Litro, impspired, etc. An independent scholar, Sultana Raza's presented papers on Romanticism (Keats) and Fantasy (Tolkien) in international conferences.

Jim Simpson (Page 256)

James Simpson, from the North of Ireland began writing literary fiction in 2010. An Irish Novel Fair winner, his work has been broadcast on national radio. In 2021 he published Smokes and Birds, a collection of short stories. He holds a Masters in Creative Writing from the Seamus Heaney Centre, Belfast.

William Ogden Haynes (Page 260)

William Ogden Haynes is a poet and author of short fiction from Alabama who was born in Michigan. He has published nine collections of poetry (Points of Interest, Uncommon Pursuits, Remnants, Stories in Stained Glass, Carvings, Going South, Contemplations, Time on My Hands and The Works) and one book of short stories (Youthful Indiscretions) all available on Amazon.com. Over 200 of his poems and short stories have appeared in literary journals and his work is frequently anthologized. http://www.williamogdenhaynes.com

Patricia M Osborne (Page 266)

Patricia M Osborne is married with grown-up children and grandchildren. In 2019 she graduated with an MA in Creative Writing. She is a published novelist, poet and short fiction writer with five poetry pamphlets published by The Hedgehog Poetry Press, and numerous poems and short stories appearing in various literary magazines and anthologies. Her debut poetry pamphlet, Taxus Baccata, was nominated for the Michael Marks Pamphlet Award.

Patricia has a successful blog at Whitewingsbooks.com featuring other writers. When Patricia isn't working on her own writing, she enjoys sharing her knowledge, acting as a mentor to fellow writers.

Jan Spooner (Page 268)

Having created since I could hold a pen, my first rejection was at aged nine. Over the years I travelled with my R.A.F. husband and taught from 4 to 40 year olds in Africa, Cyprus and Wales, hopefully transferring a love and enthusiasm of the written and spoken word.
Scribing from protest poetry to Monologues my inspiration is most fluent when creating an emotive response eg Ghost Wind.
Love the musical rhythms of Dylan Thomas in Under Milk Wood and chatted to Simon Armitage at Chelt Lit Fest.

Kac Young (Page 269)

Kac Young spent 30 years working as a producer and director in the television industry in Hollywood. She also earned three doctorates in Clinical Hypnotherapy, Naturopathy and Natural Healing. To date she has authored 27 books on self-help, spirituality, and personal growth. She was a private pilot in her early years, became a licensed Minister of Religious Science and teaches Medical Qigong for health and inner strength. Currently, she is writing a drama series for television featuring the healing power of Reiki. She is an avid animal rights supporter and a believer in equality for women worldwide.

Mal Leicester (Page 289)

Mal Leicester has a PhD in the philosophy of education and is Emeritus Professor at Nottingham University. Previously she was Senior Lecturer in Continuing Education at the University of Warwick. She has been a secondary school English teacher, a teacher trainer, Avon's advisor for Multicultural Education and Director of an anti-racist community organisation. Mal has written educational books and papers, several story anthologies for children and Jane's Journey for Imspspired. She lives in Lincolnshire with her husband Roger Twelvetrees.

Maureen Cullen (Page 294)

Maureen was born in West Dunbartonshire and now lives in Argyll and Bute. She is a retired social worker who specialised in fostering and adoption. In 2015, she gained an MA in Creative Writing from Lancaster University where she studied poetry and short fiction. She has been shortlisted in various competitions, including The V. S. Pritchett Short Story Prize, The Fish Short Story Prize and The Bristol Short Story Prize.

Shirley Bell (Page 305)

Shirley Bell is married with three adult children and three grandchildren. She is a poet, photographer and artist and she is currently studying for an MA in Fine Art. She is widely published with her poetry archived at the Special Collection in the University of Lincoln Library. She has worked for many years giving readings all over the country and running workshops for all ages. She was editor of The Blue Nib 2017-2019 and impspired magazine, until she had major health problems n 2020. Her latest book, The Benediction of Yellow, was published in 2022 by Universe Press.

Raymond Jones (Page 304)

I am a founding member of Sleaford hub writers group, and was a member of Stamford stanza group until unfortunately it closed, my work covers a broad spectrum of subjects some inspired by Nature and to a degree by Pablo Neruda. I have self-published *bee-sieged*, a book which highlights man's use of the honeybee as a weapon of war, (sold 500 copies) although not poetry, it inspired me to write more, and poetry seemed a natural progression.

Brendan Magee (Page 307)

Brendan Magee is from County Fermanagh, now a retired civil servant who served in London, Belfast, Liverpool, Manchester, and finally Coleraine where he lives. A member of North Coast and Freshfield writers Groups work includes McGarrigle's Field a play. Living Up To The Name for Flash Fiction Armagh and You Tube on 19 June 2019, also published in The Bramley Anthology vol2. The Ring in Flash Fiction Magazine published November 2019. Rescue with a flip and a smile, The Real You, Me, Her, Him, Still Serving launched in Irish Hares and Seahorses 4 May 2022.

Polly Richardson (Page 329)

Polly Richardson (Munnelly) Polly is a Dublin born poet now living and writing on the Dingle Peninsula, Kerry, Ireland. She has been published both nationally and internationally in many anthologies and e-zines under the surname of Munnelly and more recently Richardson. A contributing poet to US-based poetry forum Mad Swirl and Europe's Live Encounters digi mag with poems featuring in Boston's Nixes Mate review, Porter Gulch Review Cabrillo college US, Italian based Lotus Eater mag and member of and co-runs Navan creative writers group: The Bulls Arse. She has been heard reading at national and international poetry festivals from 2013 to 2019 including Trim's (Meath Ireland) first poetry festival in 2019. Her debut collection Winters Breath was launched with Impspired early September 2020.

Printed in Great Britain
by Amazon

85258691R00210